fast &fun
knits

fast &fun knits

Claire Garland

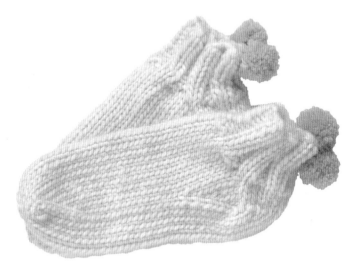

D&C
David and Charles
www.rucraft.co.uk

A DAVID & CHARLES BOOK
© F&W Media International, LTD 2011

David & Charles is an imprint of F&W Media International, LTD
Brunel House, Forde Close, Newton Abbot, TQ12 4PU, UK

F&W Media International, LTD is a subsidiary of F+W Media, Inc.
4700 East Galbraith Road, Cincinnati, OH 45236

First published in the UK and USA in 2011

ISBN-13: 978-0-7153-3869-8 paperback
ISBN-10: 0-7153-3869-2 paperback

Printed in China by RR Donnelley
for F&W Media International LTD,
Brunel House, Forde Close, Newton Abbot, TQ12 4PU, UK

10 9 8 7 6 5 4 3 2 1

Publisher Alison Myer
Acquisitions Editor Jennifer Fox-Proverbs
Editor James Brooks
Project editor Kate Haxell

Pattern checker Marilyn Wilson
Senior Designer Victoria Marks
Photographer Karl Adamson
Senior Production Controller Kelly Smith

David & Charles publish high quality books on a wide range of subjects.
For more great book ideas visit: **www.rucraft.co.uk**

A table, a chair, a bowl of fruit and a violin;
what else does a man need to be happy?
– *Albert Einstein*

A table, a (comfy) chair, a bar of chocolate and
some yarn and knitting needles;
what else do I need to be happy?
– *Claire Garland.*

Dedicated to like-minded philosophers!

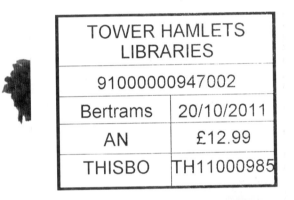

Contents

Introduction

I have fun when I am knitting – such a simple thing to say, and so very true.

I love to create things; I suppose it's in my nature, but when I am making something from yarn I feel so very positive and content. Yarn is warm and soft, yarn is colourful and textural, and the meditative process of interlacing and looping is very satisfactory indeed. Plus, added to those feel-good factors, you also end up with something that brings pleasure to you and – if you make items as gifts to share the pleasure – to those around you. How could you not be happy with that?

This process of making yourself feel comforted and content by creating something from yarn is in essence the very nature of this book. This is a 'quick fix to happiness' (all the projects are designed to be completed in a day), feel-good factor pattern book, where a warmth and sense of cheer and fun pervade every mood-boosting knitted project.

Each item has been carefully designed to give you the maximum feeling of optimism and joy. Each project reflects a positive mood, from its bold, bright, happy and cheery colour palette to its quirkiness, quickness, cosiness, fun-loving or inspirational appeal.

HAPPY YARNS

Each project tells you how much of what type of yarn you'll need to knit it, and you'll find a list of the yarns I used at the back of the book. I've selected yarns that suit the mood of the project, both in colour and texture, but you can use any yarn that inspires you, as long as it fits the requirements given.

Colour is such a feel-good thing that it's really worth spending time choosing the perfect tone for your project. And there's so much yarn to choose from.

For accessories, choose colours that match outfits or suit your skin and hair so that you'll wear and wear the items you knit. Interior projects can be matched to an existing scheme – or you can just knit everything in your favourite colours and love doing so.

Deliciously soft yarns are lovely to handle and are perfect for most of these projects, though some items, such as the FENG SHUI PURSE, need a fairly hardwearing yarn or they won't last very long.

QUICK KNITS

It's lovely to get speedy results,
especially when they don't skimp
on style. With these projects
you can pick up your needles
and yarn in the morning, and be
happily enjoying your new piece
in the evening.

Going to a party tonight? Knit
yourself a TWINKLE NECKLACE
to match your outfit. Planning
an evening in front of the telly?
Knit a pair of TOASTY TOES the
snuggliest slipper socks
to keep tootsies warm on
winter evenings.

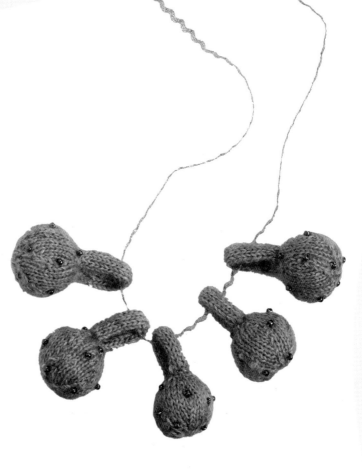

FEEL-GOOD DESIGNS

Let me tempt you with a few examples…

COOL HEAD HAT these super speedy projects are a joy to knit of an evening. They are knitted in the round on double-pointed needles – a very therapeutic knitting method – and are created in cool colours to calm and soothe the furrowed brow and lift and lighten the mood, each with an added fun element to cheer up the dullest, coldest day.

GIVE A WAVE MITTS are fingerless favourites in hot colours radiating a sense of comfort, bestowing a warm greeting on everyone who meets you.

FUN FRUIT and MONSTER HAPPY will bring a smile and a giggle – laughter and wit bring instant happiness.

COSY COVERINGS combine knitted cosiness with jaunty fabric in tones reminiscent of the scent of summer lavender, bringing comfort and homely joy.

And my favourite project, HUG A MUG COSY; chocolate, tea and coffee cup cosies brimming with happiness and warmth inside and out!

I was more than happy to make each and every one of these projects and, using only one or two balls of yarn for each project, happy to be thrifty.

Bring joy to yourself and keep fun & fast knitting!

Claire Garland

HOMESTYLE SMILE

Cosy coverings

A happy medium

A pair of projects that is perfect for the sofa. The sewing is all very simple, so no need to panic about that, and the knitting is equally stress-free. The combination of the two items not only looks great, but they are almost as relaxing to make as they are to snuggle up with once the pieces are finished.

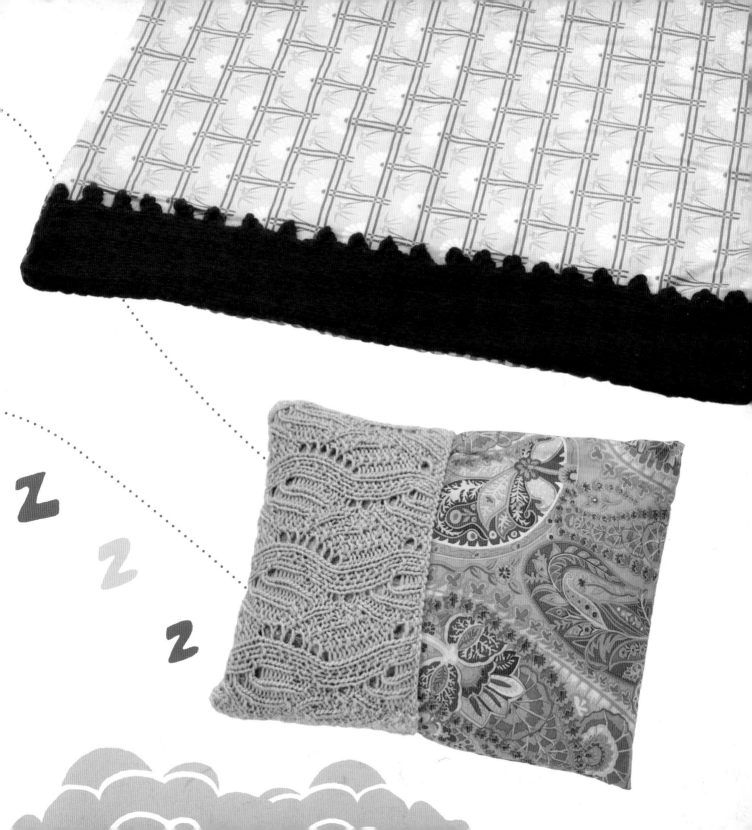

Cosy quilt

Lovely as a lap quilt or a car quilt, the yarn trim is cloud soft.

YOU WILL NEED

Yarn
1 x 3½oz (100g) ball bulky-weight (chunky) yarn – minimum 87yds (80m)

Needles
2 x size 15 (10mm) knitting needles

Notions
Knitter's sewing needle

Top fabric measuring:
47½ x 38in (120 x 96cm)

Backing fabric measuring:
47½ x 38in (120 x 96cm)

Batting (wadding) measuring 46½ x 37in (118 x 94cm) (a blanket cut to size or a cot duvet the right size)

Dressmakers' pins and tacking thread and needle

Sewing machine and sewing thread

Quilters' pins, thread and needle

Dressmakers' chalk

Gauge (Tension)
9 rows and 8½ sts to 4in (10cm) over st st using size 15 (10mm) needles

Finished size
Approx. 46½ x 37in (118 x 94cm)

Happy yarn
This chunky yarn is lovely to handle AND it knits up really quickly – an absolutely ideal combination!

Knitting notes

As you simply repeat the pattern until the knitting is the required size, it is easy to substitute a different yarn if you want to. Knit a swatch in the new yarn and if you feel that the panel isn't wide enough, simply increase the number of stitches, making sure you cast on an even number. You can also cast on and bind (cast) off more stitches for the picots, though it must be an odd number each time.

Stitch 'n' smile

As you are knitting, congratulate yourself on choosing a blanket project that will be finished before you're bored with it (unlike some all-knit blankets that go on and on and on…).

GET KNITTING

Loosely cast on 16 sts using size 15 (10mm) needles.

Row 1 Bind (cast) off 3 sts, k to end. (13 sts)

Row 2 P.

Row 3 K1, *sl1, k1, rep from * to end.

Row 4 P.

Row 5 Cast on 3 sts, bind (cast) off 3 sts, k to end.

Rep last 4 rows until the knitted panel measures the width of the quilt.

Bind (cast) off.

GET MAKING

Right sides together and taking ½in (1cm) seam allowances, join top of quilt to backing, first pinning, then basting (tacking), then machine sewing all around. Leave a 12in (30cm) gap in the lower edge for turning through and inserting the batting (wadding). Turn quilt right side out.

Insert the batting (wadding), if necessary following the manufacturer's guidelines on which way up and whether you need to iron it first. Make sure the wadding reaches each corner of the quilt.

Quilt-top facing and starting from the centre, insert pins to sandwich the quilt together at regular 6in (15cm) intervals; depending on the nature of the pattern of your quilt you may need to measure and mark out the spacing.

Hand-sew a couple of short stitches at each pin to quilt the layers together. Remove the pin.

Thread a short length of knitting yarn through each stitch and tie it in a decorative knot.

Making up

On the knitted trim, weave in ends and press carefully. Sew the trim to the quilt top, working blanket stitch along the top edge and down the cast on and bound (cast) off edges.

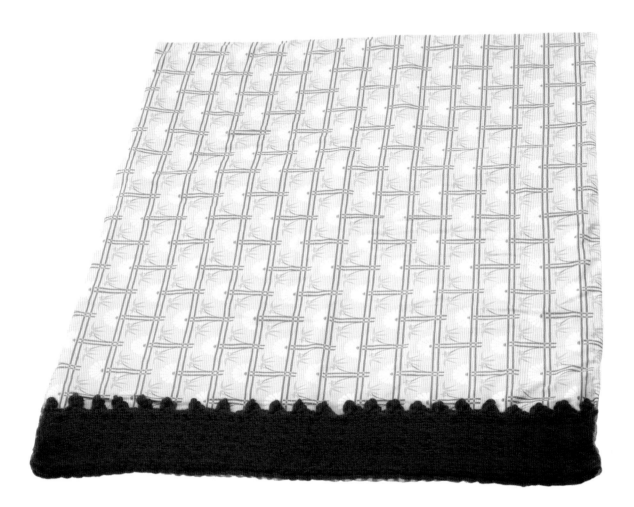

Stitch 'n' smile

You can spend happy hours mixing and matching your lace panel and a printed fabric. There's a huge range of fabrics to choose from, so take the knitted lace with you to the shops and indulge yourself in blissful fabric shopping.

Snuggle pillow

You can sew the knitted panel over an existing cushion or a bespoke one – the instructions for a basic fabric cushion are given here.

YOU WILL NEED

Yarn
1 x 1¾oz (50g) ball sport-weight (DK) yarn – minimum 113yds (105m)

Needles
2 x size 10½ (7mm) knitting needles

Notions
Knitter's sewing needle

Dressmakers' pins

Sewing machine, thread and needle

Cushion (or cushion pad) measuring 16½in (42cm) x 12½in (32cm)

20 x 20in (50 x 50cm) of fabric if you are making your own cushion – this can be a single piece or made up of patches, it depends how you want your cushion to look

Gauge (Tension)
29 rows and 20 sts to 4in (10cm) over st st, 14 sts to 4in (10cm) over patt sts, using size 10½ (7mm) needles

Finished size
The panel width fits a cushion pad 12½in (32cm) wide (see Knitting Notes)

Happy yarn
Lilacs and mauves are thought of as calming, relaxing colours, ideal for an indulgent evening snuggled in your cosy coverings doing nothing except watching a great film (and maybe eating some chocolates).

Special instructions and tips
To work how much yarn you will need to complete a whole row, spread the knitting out flat and measure the width of a row. Multiply this measurement by three and add on a few inches (centimetres) for weaving in.

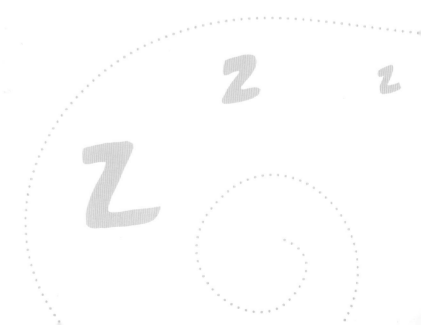

Knitting notes

You may want to add lace trims, buttons, floral corsages, anything that takes your fancy – this is your cushion! However, do bear practicality in mind and don't add anything spiky or precious to a cushion that is going to get squashed on the sofa.

If you want to make the panel wider to fit a different-sized cushion pad, then add multiples of 10 stitches to the pattern. Always knit a test swatch to make sure that your adjusted pattern will fit your cushion.

Stitch 'n' smile

For an even cosier cushion – with no more effort, I hasten to add – replace the cotton fabric part of the cushion with a vintage blanket or an old recycled, or felted, sweater.

GET KNITTING

Cast on 43 sts using size 10½ (7mm) needles very loosely.

Row 1 (WS) [P3, yo, skpo, k1, p1, k1, p1, k1] 4 times, p3.

Row 2 P3, [p3, k1, p3, k1, p1, k1] 4 times.

Row 3 [P3, yo, p1, skpo, p1, k1, p1, k1] 4 times, p3.

Row 4 P3, [p3, k1, p1, k1, p1, k1, p1, k1] 4 times.

Row 5 [P3, yo, k1, p1, skpo, k1, p1, k1] 4 times, p3.

Row 6 P3, [p4, k1, p1, k2, p1, k1] 4 times.

Row 7 [P3, yo, p1, k1, p1, skpo, p1, k1] 4 times, p3.

Row 8 P3, [p3, k1, p1, k3, p1, k1] 4 times.

Row 9 [P3, yo, p2, k1, p1, skpo, k1] 4 times, p3.

Row 10 P3, [p2, k1, p1, k1, p1, k2] 4 times.

Row 11 [P3, yo, p1, k1, p1, k1, p1, skpo] 4 times, p3.

Row 12 P3, [p3, k1, p1, k1, p1, k1, p1, k1] 4 times.

Row 13 [P3, k1, p1, k1, p1, k1, k2tog, yo] 4 times, p3.

Row 14 P3, [k1, p2, k1, p1, k1, p1, k1, p1, k1] 4 times.

Row 15 [P3, k1, p1, k1, p1, k2tog p1, yo] 4 times, p3.

Row 16 P3, [p1, k1, p1, k1, p1, k1, p1, k1, p1, k1] 4 times.

Row 17 [P3, k1, p1, k1, k2tog, p1, k1, yo] 4 times, p3.

Row 18 P3, [p2, k1, p2, k1, p1, k1, p1, k1] 4 times.

Row 19 [P3, k1, p1, k2tog, p1, k1, p1, yo] 4 times, p3.

Row 20 P3, [p3, k1, p1, k1, p1, k1, p1, k1] 4 times.

Row 21 [P3, k1, k2tog, p1, k1, p1, k1, yo] 4 times, p3.

Row 22 P3, [p2, k1, p1, k1, p2, k1, p1, k1] 4 times.

Row 23 [P3, k2tog, p1, k1, p1, k1, p1, yo] 4 times, p3.

Row 24 P3, [p3, k1, p1, k1, p1, k1, p1, k1] 4 times.

These 24 rows form the lace patt. Cont with patt until the almost all the yarn is used, leaving enough yarn to bind (cast) off with very loosely – see Special Instructions and Tips.

Stitch 'n' smile

This isn't a complicated lace pattern, so don't be scared of the instructions. If you haven't knitted lace before, then practise the pattern with some spare yarn before you start. If you've got a row counter it will help you keep track of your place in the pattern.

GET MAKING

Cut the fabric into two panels that measure the same size as your cushion pad plus ½in (1cm) seam allowances all around. Right sides facing, pin the pieces of fabric together. Sew around the edge, leaving a gap large enough to insert the cushion pad. Turn the cover to RS. Insert the cushion pad and sew the gap closed.

Making up

On the knitted panel, weave in ends at bound (cast) off and cast on edges. Stretch the panel over one end of your cushion and slip-stitch it in place using spare yarn or matching sewing thread. Embellish at will!

Lovely lights

A happy medium

Pop an electric tealight into a glass candle holder and then slip on a pretty knitted cover to make a magical lantern. Hang lanterns in trees to create the loveliest evening light for mid-summer picnics and autumnal parties. At Christmas the lanterns will look festive hung around the home or laid along the mantelpiece.

Tassel lantern

An elegant, lacy lantern with a beaded tassel tail.

YOU WILL NEED

Yarn
1 x 1¾oz (50g) ball sport-weight (DK) yarn – minimum 136yds (125m); this amount makes two lanterns

Needles
4 x size 2 (3mm) double-pointed knitting needles

Notions
2 x 14oz (324ml) glass candle holders, jam jars, confit jars or glass tumblers, approx. 3in (8cm) diameter at the top x 4in (10cm) high

Knitter's sewing needle

4 x beads for the tie and the tassel

Card and spare yarn to make the tassel

Gauge (Tension)
22 rows and 30 sts to 4in (10cm) over st st using size 2 (3mm) needles

Finished size
Approx. 3½in (9cm) diameter at base x 5in (13cm) high

Happy yarn
Smooth cotton yarn shows stitch detail beautifully and is perfect for this little, elegant project.

Knitting notes
Experiment with really fine yarns for these lanterns – a spider's-web thin yarn, such Rowan Kid Silk Haze, would make a beautifully ethereal lantern. You may need to knit with the yarn doubled to make it strong enough to hold a glass jar.

A group of different-sized lanterns, knitted in different-weight yarns and in different colours, would look stunning when arranged together.

These lanterns also make simple, quick-to-knit gifts for friends and family.

Stitch 'n' smile

These covers are really quick to make and are a great way of using up odd balls of yarn from your stash. And all knitters love stash-busting projects!

GET KNITTING

Cast on 77 sts using size 2 (3mm) needles.
Slip 77 sts p-wise and divide: 26 sts on n1, 25 sts on n2, 26 sts on n3.
With RS facing, keeping gauge (tension) fairly tight on first rnd, work in the rnd as follows:
Rnd 1 K77.
Place marker to mark beg of rnd.
Rep last rnd 4 times more.
Rnd 6 *K2, yo, p1, p3tog, p1, yo, rep from * to marker.
Rnds 7–9 K77.
Rep last 4 rnds twice more.
Rnd 18 *K2, yo, p1, p3tog, p1, yo, rep from * to marker.
Rnd 19 [K2tog, k5] 11 times. (66 sts)
Rnd 20–21 K66.
Rnd 22 *K1, yo, p1, p3tog, p1, yo, rep from * to marker.
Rnd 23–25 K66.
Rep last 4 rnds twice more.
Rnd 34 *K1, yo, p1, p3tog, p1, yo, rep from * to marker.
Rnd 35 [k4, k2tog] 11 times. (55 sts)
Rnd 36–37 K55.
Rnd 38 *Yo, p1, p3tog, p1, rep from * to end. (44 sts)
Rnd 39 K44.
Rep last rnd 5 times more.
Cut yarn and thread end through sts. Pull to gather up, creating the base of lantern, and secure the yarn.

Hanging loop

Cast on 4 sts using size 2 (3mm) needles.
Row 1 K4.
Work as i-cord as follows:
Slide sts to other end of needle without turning. Pull working yarn across back of i-cord.
Cont to work i-cord until the hanging loop measures approx. 19in (48cm).
Bind (cast) off.

Tie

Cast on 2 sts using size 2 (3mm) needles.
Row 1 K2.
Work as i-cord as follows:
Slide sts to other end of needle without turning. Pull working yarn across back of i-cord.
Cont to work i-cord until the tie measures approx. 19in (48cm).
Cut yarn and thread end through sts. Pull up tight and secure.

Tassel

Cut a piece of card 4¾ x 2in (12 x 5cm) with a slot ¾in (2cm) down from one short edge, the slot measuring 1¼in (3cm) wide x ¼in (6mm) deep.
Place a length of yarn approx. 12in (30cm) long across the top of the card, about halfway between the top of the card and the top of the slot (cut small snips in the edges of the card to hold yarn in place) – this will be used to tie the top of the tassel.
Wind yarn around the card from top to bottom over the slot, about 20 times or to desired tassel fullness.
Thread a length of yarn through the slot and tie it tightly around the tassel to form the head. Knot twice more.
Using the length of yarn placed in slits at the top of the card, tie around the top of the tassel.
Cut the yarn at the bottom of the tassel with sharp scissors. Slide the tassel off the card.
Fluff up the tassel. If strands are uneven, just trim them.
Attach a couple of beads to the top of the tassel, then sew the tassel to the bottom of the lantern cover.

Making up

Slip the candle holder (or jam jar) into the lantern cover. Sew the ends of the hanging loop very securely to the inside at the top edge of the lantern cover – making sure they are opposite each other. Weave the cord tie in and out of the holes (beginning and ending in the same hole) created in the lacy pattern around the top of the lantern cover. Pull up to gather around the candle holder. Thread a bead onto each end of the tie and knot to hold them in place. Pop an electric tea-light into the base of the holder.

Button lanterns

A couple of vintage buttons add a retro twist to the lanterns.

YOU WILL NEED

Yarn
1 x 1¾oz (50g) ball sport-weight (DK) yarn – minimum 136yds (125m); this amount makes two lanterns

Needles
4 x size 2 (3mm) double-pointed knitting needles

Notions
2 x 14oz (324ml) glass candle holders, jam jars, confit jars or glass tumblers, approx. 3in (8cm) diameter at the top x 4in (10cm) high

Knitter's sewing needle

2 x buttons for the tie

Card and spare yarn to make the tassel

Gauge (Tension)
22 rows and 30 sts to 4in (10cm) over st st using size 2 (3mm) needles

Finished size
Approx. 3½in (9cm) diameter at base x 5in (13cm) high

GET KNITTING
Work lantern cover, hanging loop and tie as for Tassel Lantern.

Making up
Make up as for Tassel Lantern, but omitting tassel and tying a button to each end of the tie.

Stitch 'n' smile

For a burst of brilliant extra colour, paint the candle holders with coloured glass paints and slip on contrast knitted covers.

Fun fruit

A quirky project that, with just a change of yarn, can become one of three desirably practical items. Make the pears in realistic tones or go crazy with vivid colours for really retro, psychedelic '70s fruit.

Pear doorstop

A chunky pear to hold the door open.

YOU WILL NEED

Yarn
1 x 1¾oz (50g) ball worsted-weight
(Aran) yarn – minimum 164yds (150m)

Needles
4 x size 8 (5mm) double-pointed
knitting needles

2 x size 2 (3mm) double-pointed
knitting needles

Notions
Row marker

Toy filling

Sand, rice, lentils or similar material
to act as a ballast

2 x 5in (13cm) squares of lining fabric

Sewing needle and thread

Knitter's sewing needle

Felt – optional

Gauge (Tension)
24 rows and 18 sts to 4in (10cm) over
st st using size 8 (5mm) needles

Finished size
Approx. 8½in (22cm)
tall x 16½in (42cm)
circumference at widest part

Happy yarn
Choose a good-quality yarn that will be
hardwearing for this version of the knitted pear.

Special instructions and tips
To make the stalk stiffer, 'paint' on a weak mix of PVA glue
and water and leave to dry. The leaves are sewn on to the
stalk before stiffening.

The ballast sits at the base of the pear. Stuff the top of
the pear with the toy filling material, then manipulate the
stuffing and ballast material to shape the pear as desired.

Knitting notes

Go bigger with larger needles and bulky yarn for a giant pear, or use the thinnest needles you can find and crochet cotton to make a delicate, tiny fruit.

The pears would make lovely Christmas tree decorations when knitted in white or silver. Add a few cloves to the stuffing give them a festive scent.

Stitch 'n' smile

If you want to add a little whimsical texture to your fruit, try combining a single strand of mohair yarn with the main yarn for an appealingly fluffy finish.

GET KNITTING

Begin by making a lining bag for the ballast. Simply sew together around all four edges of the fabric squares, leaving a gap for filling. Use a funnel to fill the bag loosely with ballast material, then sew the gap closed.

Cast on 3 sts using size 8 (5mm) needles.

**Row 1 [Kfb] 3 times. (6 sts)

Slip 6 sts p-wise and divide equally over 3 needles.

With RS facing, keeping gauge (tension) fairly tight on first rnd, work in the rnd as follows:

Rnd 2 [Kfb] 6 times. (12 sts)

Rnd 3 [K1, kfb] 6 times. (18 sts)

Rnd 4 K18.

Place marker to mark beg of rnd.

Rep last rnd 9 times more.

Rnd 14 [K2, kfb] 6 times. (24 sts)

Rnd 15 K24.

Rep last rnd twice more.

Rnd 18 [K3, kfb] 6 times. (30 sts)

Rnd 19 K30.

Rep last rnd 3 times more.

Rnd 23 [K4, kfb] 6 times. (36 sts)

Rnd 24 K36.

Rep last rnd 4 times more.

Rnd 29 [K5, kfb] 6 times. (42 sts)

Rnd 30 K42.

Rep last rnd 4 times more.

Rnd 35 *K2, [kfb, k1] 5 times, k2, rep from * twice more. (57 sts)

Rnd 36 K57.

Rep last rnd 7 times more.

Rnd 44 *K2, [kfb, k2] 5 times, kfb, k1, rep from * twice more. (75 sts)

Rnd 45 K75.

Rep last rnd 7 times more.

Rnd 53 [K3, k2tog] 15 times. (60 sts)

Rnd 54 K60.

Rep last rnd twice more.

Rnd 57 [K2, k2tog] 15 times. (45 sts)

Rnd 58 K45.

Rep last rnd twice more.

Rnd 61 [K1, k2tog] 15 times. (30 sts)

Rnd 62 K30.

Rep last rnd twice more. At this stage insert the ballast; push it up towards the top of the pear as you complete the knitting. Stuff the pear well with toy filling into the top of the pear and around the ballast.

Rnd 63 [K2tog] 15 times. (15 sts)

Cut yarn and thread end through rem sts. Pull up tight and secure by threading the tail end back into the main body, taking care not to puncture the ballast bag, at the same time pulling tight to create the dimple in the base.

Homestyle smile | Fun fruit

Stalk

Cast on 5 sts using size 8 (5mm) needles.

Rnd 1 K5.

Work as i-cord as follows:
Slide sts to other end of needle without turning. Pull working yarn across back of i-cord.

Rnd 2 K5.

Rnd 3 K2tog, k1, k2tog. (3 sts)
Cont to work i-cord until the cord measures approx. 2in (5cm).
Leave a long tail end, cut yarn and thread end through sts. Sew the stalk to the top of the pear using the tail end, at the same time pushing in the tip of the pear to create the dimple at the top.**

Knitted leaf

Using a small amount of sport-weight (DK) yarn in a leafy shade of green and a pair of size 2 (3mm) double-pointed needles, put slip knot loosely on needle, kfb into slip knot, then before slipping the new stitch off the needle, knit the stitch again. (3 sts)

K3, work as i-cord over next 8 rnds.
Cont to work in st st.

Row 9 Cast on 2 sts, k to end. (5 sts)

Row 10 Cast on 2 sts, p to end. (7 sts)

Row 11 Kfb, k to last st, kfb. (9 sts)

Row 12 P.

Rep last 2 rows twice more. (13 sts)
Work 8 rows st st, ending with a p row.

Row 25 K2tog, k to end. (12 sts)

Row 26 P2tog, p to end. (11 sts)

Rep last 2 rows 4 times more. (3 sts)

Row 35 K2tog, k1. (2 sts)

Break yarn, thread end through rem 2 sts, weave in end.
If necessary press the leaf flat.

Making up

Sew the leaf to the stalk. Stiffen the stalk as suggested in Special Instructions and Tips if required. Embroider short stitches over the pear to add texture.

Stitch 'n' smile

If you prefer you can make almost instant leaves for your pear by cutting shapes from felt and then sewing them to the stalk. This is also the best way to make leaves for the smaller paperweight and pincushion pears.

Pear paperweight

A medium pear to help keep your desk organised.

YOU WILL NEED

Yarn
1 x 1¾oz (50g) ball sport-weight (DK) yarn – minimum 127yds (116m)

Small amount of sport-weight (DK) yarn in darker colour for markings

Needles
4 x size 4 (3.5mm) double-pointed knitting needles

Notions
Row marker

Toy filling

Sand, rice, lentils or similar material to act as a ballast; you could use a flat pebble in the fabric bag.

2 x 5in (13cm) squares of lining fabric

Sewing needle and thread

Knitter's sewing needle

Felt

Gauge (Tension)
28 rows and 21 sts to 4in (10cm) over st st using size 4 (3.5mm) needles

Finished size
Approx. 6¼in (16cm) tall x 14¼in (36cm) circumference at widest part

Happy yarn
Make this in a gorgeously soft yarn and you'll love to pick it up and play while you ponder your paperwork.

GET KNITTING
Make a ballast bag as for the Pear Doorstop. Cast on 3 sts using size 4 (3.5mm) needles. Cont to work as Pear Doorstop from ** to **, altering needle sizes accordingly.

Making up
Using a length of darker yarn, work small stitches randomly over the pear for decoration.
Cut out a leaf from felt and sew it to the stalk. Stiffen the stalk as suggested in Special Instructions and Tips if required.

Stitch 'n' smile

Instead of using the pear as a paperweight you could fill it with potpourri or dab scented oil onto the lining to create an aromatic pear to hang in your car, wardrobe or bathroom.

Pear pincushion

A little prickly pear to hold your pins.

YOU WILL NEED

Yarn
1 x 1¾oz (50g) ball sport-weight (DK) yarn – minimum 130yds (120m)

Needles
4 x size 2 (2.75mm) double-pointed knitting needles

Notions
Row marker

Toy filling

Sand, rice, lentils or similar material to act as a ballast; for the pear pincushion use sand, which sharpens the pins as they are inserted into the cushion

2 x 3in (8cm) square of lining fabric

Sewing needle and thread

Knitter's sewing needle

Felt

Gauge (Tension)
37 rows and 28 sts to 4in (10cm) over st st using size 2 (2.75mm) needles

Finished size
Approx. 4¾in (12cm) tall x 10¾in (27cm) circumference at widest part

Happy yarn
Variegated yarn is a really easy way to add different tones to your knitted pear. It's always great when the yarn does the work for you!

GET KNITTING
Make a ballast bag as for the Pear Doorstop. Cast on 3 sts using size 2 (2.75mm) needles. Cont to work as Pear Doorstop from ** to **, altering needle sizes accordingly.

Making up
Cut out a leaf from felt and sew it to the stalk. Stiffen the stalk as suggested in Special Instructions and Tips if required.

Stitch 'n' smile

Choose pretty pins with glass or pearlised heads to make your pincushion extra-lovely.

WEAR A HUG

Cool head hat

So cute, this non-itchy winter hat is simple to knit, looks cool yet keeps heads warm, and fits children up to ten years old. There are three different toppers to choose from – a pom-pom, a knot or a knitted bell.

Pom-pom hat

This hat is topped with 'ears' joined by a perky pom-pom.

YOU WILL NEED

Yarn
2 x 1¾oz (50g) balls worsted-weight (Aran) yarn – minimum 175yds (160m)

Needles
4 x size 7 (4.5mm) double-pointed knitting needles

Notions
Row marker

Knitter's sewing needle

Pom-pom maker

Gauge (Tension)
24 rows and 16 sts to 4in (10cm) over st st using size 7 (4.5mm) needles

Finished size
Fits babies to 10-year olds

Happy yarn
Make sure you choose a yarn that is soft against the skin, as no child will happily wear an itchy hat!

Special instructions and tips
The nature of the hat enables it to fit different-sized heads: choosing a fibre containing about 20% nylon makes for a stretchy yarn, and as you knit the cast on edge naturally rolls up to create the brim of the hat, which can be rolled up further to suit a smaller head.

Knitting notes

You could make any kind of pixie hat using this basic pattern. Once you have got to round 47, you can go on to knit one of the three toppers shown, or invent your own. Tapering the top with gradual decreases will create a pointy pixie hat, which knitted in red with a white pom-pom makes a perfect Santa hat!

Stitch 'n' smile
Self-striping yarns can make fabulously fun hats, with stripes that get wider as the number of stitches decreases.

GET KNITTING

**Cast on 90 sts using size 7 (4.5mm) needles.
Slip 90 sts p-wise and divide equally over 3 needles.
With RS facing, keeping gauge (tension) fairly tight
on first rnd, work in the rnd as follows:
Rnd 1 K90.
Place marker to mark beg of rnd.
Rnd 2 P90.
Rep last 2 rnds once more.
Rnd 5 P1, k to marker.
Rep last rnd 42 times more or until hat measures
approximately 8in (20cm).**

SHAPE EARS

Rnd 48 P1, k9, slip last 20 sts (10 from end of last rnd)
off needles and onto a piece of spare yarn, cont to
k next 45 sts, slip last 20 sts off needles and onto a
piece of spare yarn, k next 25 sts. (The front and the
back of the hat sts held on the spare yarn will
be grafted together later.)

LEFT EAR

Work back and forth in rows on first 25 sts as follows:
****Row 49 (WS)** P2tog, p to last 2 sts, p2tog. (23 sts)
Row 50 K2tog, k to last 2 sts, k2tog. (21 sts)
Rep last 2 rows 4 times more, then the first of them
again. (3 sts).
Break yarn, thread through rem 3 sts, pull up tight
and secure the end.**

RIGHT EAR

WS facing, rejoin yarn to 25 sts for Right Ear.
Work as for Left Ear from ** to **.
Slip sts from front onto a needle, slip sts from back
onto a second. Securing a long length of yarn at the
back of the work, with WS together hold needles
parallel. Work Kitchener st to close the seam, taking
off last st p-wise.

Making up

Weave in ends. Sew up ear seams using mattress
stitch. Make small pom-pom using pom-pom maker.
Sew one tail of yarn used for tying pom-pom to tip of
each ear to join them.

Stitch 'n' smile
You can make the pom-pom as large or small as you
wish, or make it in a bright contrast colour for added fizz.

Knot hat

Knit a long top for your hat and tie it into a neat knot.

YOU WILL NEED

FOR EACH HAT

Yarn
2 x 1¾oz (50g) balls worsted-weight (Aran) yarn – minimum 175yds (160m)

Needles
4 x size 7 (4.5mm) double-pointed knitting needles

Notions
Row marker

Knitter's sewing needle

Jingle bell (for bobble hat only, optional)

Gauge (Tension)
24 rows and 16 sts to 4in (10cm) over st st using size 7 (4.5mm) needles

Finished size
Fits babies to 10-year olds

GET KNITTING

Work as for Pom-pom Hat from ** to **.

SHAPE TOP OF CROWN

Rnd 48 P1, k3, k2tog, [k4, k2tog] 14 times. (75 sts)
Rnd 49 P1, k2, k2tog, [k3, k2tog] 14 times. (60 sts)
Rnd 50 P1, k1, k2tog, [k2, k2tog] 14 times. (45 sts)
Rnd 51 P1, k2tog, [k1, k2tog] 14 times. (30 sts)

TOP KNOT SHAPING

Rnd 52 [K2tog] 15 times. (15 sts)
Rnd 53 K.
Rep last rnd 34 times more.
Rnd 88 K2tog, k11, k2tog, turn. (13 sts)
Work back and forth in rows of st st to shape the top as follows:
Row 89 P.
Row 90 K2tog, k to last 2 sts, k2tog. (11 sts)
Rep last 2 rows 5 times more. (1 st)
Fasten off.

Making up

Weave in ends. Mattress stitch across the seam on shaping. Knot the top of the hat from Top Knot Shaping.

Bobble hat

You can put a jingle bell into the bobble if you wish.

GET KNITTING

Work as for Pom-pom Hat from ** to **.

Rnd 48 P1, k13, k2tog, k14, [k14, k2tog, k14] twice. (87 sts)

Rnd 49 and foll 2 alt rnds P1, k to marker.

Rnd 50 P1, k12, k3tog, k13, [k13, k3tog, k13] twice. (81 sts)

Rnd 52 P1, k11, k3tog, k12 [k12, k3tog, k12] twice. (75 sts)

Rnd 54 P1, k2, k2tog, [k3, k2tog] 14 times. (60 sts)

Rnd 55 P1, k2, k2tog, [k3, k2tog] 11 times. (48 sts)

Rnd 56 P1, k3, k2tog, [k4, k2tog] 7 times. (40 sts)

Rnd 57 P1, k2, k2tog, [k3, k2tog] 7 times. (32 sts)

Rnd 58 P1, k1, k2tog, [k2, k2tog] 7 times. (24 sts)

Rnd 59 P1, k2tog, [k1, k2tog] 7 times. (16 sts)

Rnd 60 P2tog, [k2tog] 7 times. (8 sts)

Rnd 61 K8.

Work as i-cord as follows:

Slide sts to other end of needle without turning. Pull working yarn across back of i-cord. Cont to work until i-cord measures approx. 5½in (14cm).

BOBBLE

Next rnd [Kfb] 8 times. (16 sts)

Next rnd K16.

Slip 16 sts p-wise and divide over 3 needles as follows: 5 sts on n1, 6 sts on n2, 5 sts on n3. With RS facing, work in the rnd as follows:

Next rnd [K1, kfb] 8 times. (24 sts)

Next rnd K24.

Next rnd [K2, kfb] 8 times. (32 sts)

Next rnd K32.

Rep last rnd once more.

Next rnd [K2, k2tog] 8 times. (24 sts)

Next rnd and foll alt rnd K to marker.

Next rnd [K1, k2tog] 8 times. (16 sts)

Next rnd [K2tog] 8 times. (8 sts)

Cut yarn, thread end through rem 8 sts.

Making up

Weave in ends. Stuff the ball with spare yarn, inserting jingle bell if wanted, pull up tight and secure yarn end.

Give a wave mitts

RATING — A feel-good challenge

These cute and cosy mitts in an easy-to-work lace pattern will become staples in your winter wardrobe. Variations with different cuff lengths make them a versatile option with all sorts of outfits.

Wrist-length mitts

Keep a pair of these in your bag for unexpected chilly days.

YOU WILL NEED

Yarn
1 x ¾oz (25g) ball fingering-weight (4-ply) yarn – minimum 115yds (105m)

Needles
4 x size 0 (2mm) double-pointed knitting needles

4 x size 3 (3¼mm) double-pointed knitting needles

Notions
Row markers

Stitch holder

Knitter's sewing needle

Gauge (Tension)
42 rows and 30 sts to 4in (10cm) over lace patt using size 3 (3¼mm) needles

Finished size
To fit an average woman's hand 5½in (14cm) long from cuff to top

Happy yarn
The Jamieson's Shetland Spindrift yarn I used is a 2-ply yarn, but it knits up like a 4-ply and it comes in lots of delicious colours.

Special instructions and tips
When working the lace pattern, try repeating each row in your head as you knit. This becomes a sort of chant/mantra and you'll soon find you will eventually know it by heart and not forget where you are in the pattern.

Knitting notes

If you want even longer mitts, just keep adding rounds of stocking stitch before you begin the lace cuff pattern at the wrist. However, if the mitts are to begin at the upper arm, for super elegance you will have to begin with more stitches. Working with the gauge (tension) given, casting on 78 sts will give you a 10¼in (26cm) cuff. You will then decrease stitches back down to 44 sts as you get past the elbow; try decreasing 2 stitches evenly on every alternate row for the next 34 rows.

Self striping or patterning 'sock' yarns would make really effective mitts, in any length.

Try adding a fluffy cuff to your mitts with a mohair or angora yarn, but omit the ribbing if you do this.

Stitch 'n' smile

The idea of knitting lace with four needles in the round might make you turn pale, but as you only have to work knit rows when working in the round, circular lace is simpler than you might think.

GET KNITTING

Cast on 44 sts using size 0 (2mm) needles.
Slip 44 sts p-wise and divide equally over 3 needles.
*With RS facing, keeping gauge (tension) fairly tight on first rnd, work in the rnd as follows:
1st rnd [K1, p1] 22 times.
Place marker to mark beg of rnd.
Rep last rib rnd 3 times more.
Change to size 3 (3¼mm) needles.**
Rnd 5 K44.
Rep last rnd once more.

LACE CUFF PATTERN

***Patt rnd 1** [K4, yo, k2tog, k1, skpo, yo, k6, yo, k2tog, k1, skpo, yo, k2] twice.
Patt rnd 2 K.
Patt rnds 3–6 Rep last 2 rnds twice more.
Patt rnd 7 [K5, yo, k3tog, yo, k8, yo, k3tog, yo, k3] twice.
Patt rnd 8 K.
Patt rnd 9 [K4, skpo, yo, k1, yo, k2tog, k6, skpo, yo, k1, yo, k2tog, k2], twice.
Patt rnd 10 K.
Patt rnd 11 [K3, skpo, yo, k3, yo, k2tog, k4, skpo, yo, k3, yo, k2tog, k1] twice.
Patt rnd 12 K.
Rep these 12 Patt rnds once more and then rep Patt rnd 1 once more.

DIVIDE FOR THUMB

Slip marker at beg of rnd, kfb, k1, M1, place marker, k42 sts to beg of rnd. (46 sts)
Next rnd K6, yo, k2tog, k1, skpo, yo, k6, yo, k2tog, k1, skpo, yo, k6, yo, k2tog, k1, skpo, yo, k6, yo, k2tog, k1, skpo, yo, k2.
Next rnd Slip marker, M1, k4, M1 at marker, slip marker, k42 to beg of rnd. (48 sts)
Next rnd K8, yo, k2tog, k1, skpo, yo, k6, yo, k2tog, k1, skpo, yo, k6, yo, k2tog, k1, skpo, yo, k6, yo, k2tog, k1, skpo, yo, k2.
Next rnd Slip marker, M1, k6, M1 at marker, slip marker, k42 to beg of rnd. (50 sts)
Next rnd K11, yo, k3tog, yo, k8, yo, k3tog, yo, k8, yo, k3tog, yo, k8, yo, k3tog, yo, k3.

Next rnd Slip marker, M1, k8, M1 at marker, slip marker, k42 to beg of rnd. (52 sts)

Next rnd K12, skpo, yo, k1, yo, k2tog, k6, skpo, yo, k1, yo, k2tog, k6, skpo, yo, k1, yo, k2tog, k6, skpo, yo, k1, yo, k2tog, k2.

Next rnd Slip marker, M1, k10, M1 at marker, slip marker, k42 to beg of rnd. (54 sts)

Next rnd K13, skpo, yo, k3, yo, k2tog, k4, skpo, yo, k3, yo, k2tog, k4, skpo, yo, k3, yo, k2tog, k4, skpo, yo, k3, yo, k2tog, k1.

Next rnd Slip marker, M1, k12, M1 at marker, slip marker, k42 to beg of rnd. (56 sts)

Next rnd K16, yo, k2tog, k1, skpo, yo, k6, yo, k2tog, k1, skpo, yo, k6, yo, k2tog, k1, skpo, yo, k6, yo, k2tog, k1, skpo, yo, k2.

Next rnd Slip marker, M1, k14, M1 at marker, slip marker, k42 to beg of rnd. (58 sts)

Next rnd K18, yo, k2tog, k1, skpo, yo, k6, yo, k2tog, k1, skpo, yo, k6, yo, k2tog, k1, skpo, yo, k6, yo, k2tog, k1, skpo, yo, k2.

Next rnd Slip marker, M1, k16, M1 at marker, slip marker, k42 to beg of rnd. (60 sts)

Next rnd K across next 18 sts between markers for thumb, leave sts on a length of spare yarn (or stitch holder), k2, yo, k2tog, k1, skpo, yo, k6, yo, k2tog, k1, skpo, yo, k6, yo, k2tog, k1, skpo, yo, k6, yo, k2tog, k1, skpo, yo, k2. (42 sts)

Next rnd Place marker to indicate beg of rnd, using backward loop method cast on 4 sts across top of thumb sts on holder, k42 to beg of rnd. (46 sts)

Next rnd K7, yo, k3tog, yo, k8, yo, k3tog, yo, k8, yo, k3tog, yo, k8, yo, k3tog, yo, k3.

Next rnd K46.

Next rnd K6, skpo, yo, k1, yo, k2tog, k6, skpo, yo, k1, yo, k2tog, k6, skpo, yo, k1, yo, k2tog, k6, skpo, yo, k1, yo, k2tog, k2.

Next rnd K46.

Next rnd K5, skpo, yo, k3, yo, k2tog, k4, skpo, yo, k3, yo, k2tog, k4, skpo, yo, k3, yo, k2tog, k4, skpo, yo, k3, yo, k2tog, k1.

Next rnd K46.

Next rnd K6, yo, k2tog, k1, skpo, yo, k6, yo, k2tog, k1, skpo, yo, k6, yo, k2tog, k1, skpo, yo, k6, yo, k2tog, k1, skpo, yo, k2

Next rnd [K1, p1] 23 times.

Rep last rib rnd 3 times more.

Bind (cast) off in rib.

Thumb

Slip 18 sts held on spare yarn onto size 3 (3¼mm) needles.

RS facing, rejoin yarn to sts to left of main hand, at thumb.

Pick up and knit 1 st at place where thumb joins hand, k next st, pass 1st st over 2nd st, k17, pick up and knit 4 sts across gap. (22 sts).

Join to work in rnd.

Next rnd [K1, p1] to end.

Rep last rib rnd 3 times more.

Bind (cast) off in rib.

Making up

Weave in ends.****

¾-length mitts

These are perfect for wearing with swing coats or capes.

YOU WILL NEED

Yarn
1 x ¾oz (25g) ball fingering-weight (4-ply) yarn – minimum 115yds (105m)

Needles
4 x size 0 (2mm) double-pointed knitting needles

4 x size 3 (3¼mm) double-pointed knitting needles

Notions
Row markers

Stitch holder

Knitter's sewing needle

Gauge (Tension)
42 rows and 30 sts to 4in (10cm) over lace patt using size 3 (3¼mm) needles

Finished size
To fit an average woman's hand 6¾in (17cm) long from cuff to top

GET KNITTING

Cast on 44 sts using size 0 (2mm) needles.
Slip 44 sts p-wise and divide equally over 3 needles.
Cont to work as Wrist-length Mitts from * to **.
Rnd 5 K44.
Rep last rnd 12 times more.
Cont to work as Wrist-length Mitts from *** to ****.

Elbow-length mitts

Add a touch of vintage glamour to your outfit with these long mitts.

YOU WILL NEED

Yarn
2 x ¾oz (25g) balls fingering-weight
(4-ply) yarn – minimum
115yds (105m)

Needles
4 x size 0 (2mm) double-pointed
knitting needles

4 x size 3 (3¼mm) double-pointed
knitting needles

Notions
Row markers

Stitch holder

Knitter's sewing needle

Gauge (Tension)
42 rows and 30 sts to 4in (10cm)
over lace patt using size 3
(3¼mm) needles

Finished size
To fit an average woman's hand
9½in (24cm) long from cuff to top

GET KNITTING

Cast on 44 sts using size 0
(2mm) needles.
Slip 44 sts p-wise and divide
equally over 3 needles.
Cont to work as Wrist-length Mitts
from * to **.
Rnd 5 K44.
Rep last rnd 40 times more.
Cont to work as Wrist-length Mitts
from *** to ****.

Stitch 'n' smile
Choose whatever colour yarn you love
best for your gloves and they'll cheer
you up on the gloomiest winter day.

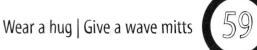

RATING  A happy medium

A perfect way to begin sock knitting; using super-soft chunky yarn and quite large needles, this easy-peasy pair is knitted up in no time. There are three length variations – short slipper length, ankle length and knee length – so choose what's right for you and get knitting!

Slipper socks

And even though the socks are short in the ankle they'll still keep your toes super-toasty!

YOU WILL NEED

Yarn
2 x 1¾oz (50g) balls bulky (chunky) yarn – minimum 41yds (38m)

Small amount of contrast yarn for pom-poms

Needles
4 x size 8 (5mm) double-pointed knitting needles

Notions
Row marker

Knitter's sewing needle

Pom-pom maker

Gauge (Tension)
21 rows and 14 sts to 4in (10cm) over st st using size 8 (5mm) needles

Finished size
To fit: average shoe size US 7 (continental 39, UK size 6) although the length is adjustable to suit; ankle circumference – 8in (20cm). For wider socks, use size 9 (5.5mm) needles.

Happy yarn
Chose a deliciously soft yarn to create luxuriously indulgent slippers.

Special instructions and tips
If you are a beginner and this is your first ever attempt at knitting a sock try using bamboo needles, the stitches are less likely to slip off these than they are off metal or plastic needles.

Kitchener Stitch is used to give the toe a 'seamless' join.

Knitting notes

Use this pattern as a basic sock pattern and add your own lace or cable detailing (there are loads of stitch patterns to chose from on the internet).

Larger needles will give you larger socks; smaller needles, smaller socks. It really is that simple!

Stitch 'n' smile

Knit socks in seasonal colours for festive feet all year around. Try red for Christmas, yellow for Easter and pumpkin orange for Halloween.

GET KNITTING

Cast on 28 sts using size 8 (5mm) needles.
Slip 28 sts p-wise and divide over three needles as
follows: 10 sts on n1, 8 sts on n2, 10 sts on n3.
With RS facing, keeping gauge (tension) fairly tight
on first rnd, work in the rnd as follows:
Rnd 1 [K2, p2] 7 times.
Place marker to mark beg of rnd.
Rep last rnd 9 times more.

**DIVIDE FOR HEEL

Next row K16 sts onto one
needle for heel, divide rem 12 sts
equally over 2 needles for instep.
Work back and forth across heel
sts only as follows:
Next row P.
Next row K.
Next row P.

TURN HEEL

Next row (RS) Sl1, k9, k2tog, k1, turn.
Next row (WS) Sl1, p5, p2tog, p1, turn.
Next row Sl1, k6, k2tog, k1, turn.
Next row Sl1, p7, p2tog, p1, turn.
Next row Sl1, k8, k2tog, turn.
Next row Sl1, p8, p2tog. (10 sts)
Next row K.
Onto new needle pick up and knit 8 sts along side of
heel, k across 6 sts from instep. Onto n2 k across 6 sts
from instep, pick up and knit 8 sts along side of heel,
onto n3 k across 10 heel sts. (38 sts)
Join into rnd and place marker to mark beg of rnd.
Next rnd Skpo, k24, k2tog, k10. (36 sts)
Next rnd K36.
Next rnd Skpo, k22, k2tog, k10. (34 sts)
Next rnd K34.
Next rnd Skpo, k20, k2tog, k10. (32 sts)
Next rnd K32.
Next rnd Skpo, k18, k2tog, k10. (30 sts)
Next rnd K30.
Next rnd Skpo, k16, k2tog, k10. (28 sts)
Next rnd K28.

Wear a hug | Toasty toes socks

WORK FOOT

Rep last rnd 33 times more, until instep, from back of heel, measures 9in (23cm) (this will eventually fit shoe size US 7/continental 39/UK size 6 – work a few more rnds for a longer sock).

SHAPE TOE

Next rnd Skpo, k14, k2tog, k10. (26 sts)
Next rnd K26.
Next rnd Skpo, k12, k2tog, k10. (24 sts)
Next rnd K24.
Next rnd Skpo, k10, k2tog, k10. (22 sts)
Next rnd K22.
Next rnd Skpo, k8, k2tog, k10. (20 sts)
Next rnd K20.
Next rnd Skpo, k6, k2tog – all onto one needle, skpo, k6, k2tog across sts from n3 (heel). (16 sts)
Leaving a long tail end, cut yarn, leave sts on needle.

Making up

With WS together, hold needles parallel. Work Kitchener Stitch to close the seam, taking off last st p-wise.
Using pom-pom maker and contrast yarn, make four small pom-poms and sew two to back of heel on each sock.
Weave in ends.**

Stitch 'n' smile

Knit these socks in a friend's favourite colour and package them in matching tissue paper and ribbon for a special gift.

Ankle socks

Wear these with Birkenstocks for boho style.

YOU WILL NEED

Yarn
2 x 1¾oz (50g) balls bulky (chunky) yarn – minimum 49yds (45m)

Small amount of contrast yarn for toes

Needles
4 x size 8 (5mm) double-pointed knitting needles

Notions
Row marker

Knitter's sewing needle

Gauge (Tension)
21 rows and 14 sts to 4in (10cm) over st st using size 8 (5mm) needles

Finished size
To fit: average shoe size US 7 (continental 39, UK size 6) although the length is adjustable to suit; ankle circumference – 8in (20cm). For wider socks, use size 9 (5.5mm) needles.

GET KNITTING

Cast on 28 sts using size 8 (5mm) needles.
Slip 28 sts p-wise and divide over three needles as follows: 10 sts on n1, 8 sts on n2, 10 sts on n3.
With RS facing, keeping gauge (tension) fairly tight on first rnd, work in the rnd as follows:
Rnd 1 [K2, p2] 7 times.
Place marker to mark beg of rnd.
Rep last rnd 11 times more.
Next rnd K.
Rep last rnd 5 times more.
Work as for Slipper Sock from ** to **, working last 3 rounds in contrast yarn and using that yarn to finish toes.

Long socks

To keep you warm in the coldest winter weather.

YOU WILL NEED

Yarn
4 x 1¾oz (50g) balls bulky (chunky) yarn – minimum 46yds (42m)

Small amount of contrast sport-weight (DK) yarn for snowflakes

Needles
4 x size 8 (5mm) double-pointed knitting needles

Notions
Row marker

Knitter's sewing needle

Gauge (Tension)
21 rows and 14 sts to 4in (10cm) over st st using size 8 (5mm) needles

Finished size
To fit: average shoe size US 7 (continental 39, UK size 6) although the length is adjustable to suit; ankle circumference approx. 8in (20cm). For wider socks, use size 9 (5.5mm) needles.

GET KNITTING

Cast on 28 sts using size 8 (5mm) needles.
Slip 28 sts p-wise and divide over three needles as follows: 10 sts on n1, 8 sts on n2, 10 sts on n3.
With RS facing, keeping gauge (tension) fairly tight on first rnd, work in the rnd as follows:
Rnd 1 [K2, p2] 7 times.
Place marker to mark beg of rnd.
Rep last rnd 11 times more.
Next rnd K.
Rep last rnd 32 times more.
Work as for Slipper Sock from ** to **.
To add snowflakes, use contrast yarn to embroider six fly stitches with extended 'arms', radiating out from a centre point.

ACCESSORISE WITH GLEE

Twinkle necklace

RATING   Fast-track fun

Chunky, arty and bold accessories to adorn yourself with, and so versatile in design. Using these simple, basic patterns you can make bracelets, belts, headbands, a chunky ring… and use absolutely any yarn from thin and silky to chunky and woolly – endless choices!

Beaded beads

String as many of these beads as you want on pretty ribbon.

YOU WILL NEED

Yarn
1 x 3½oz (100g) ball lace-weight (2-ply) yarn – minimum 874yds (800m) – used double this amount will make lots and lots of beads!

Needles
4 x size 2 (3mm) double-pointed knitting needles

Notions
Row marker

Seed beads

Sewing needle and thread

Ribbon or braid to thread knitted beads on to

Gauge (Tension)
27 rows and 35 sts to 4in (10cm) over st st using size 2 (3mm) needles

Finished size
A bead measures approximately 1¼in (3cm) in diameter

Happy yarn
You can use any yarn of the right weight, but check that it isn't itchy or your necklace won't be very comfortable to wear.

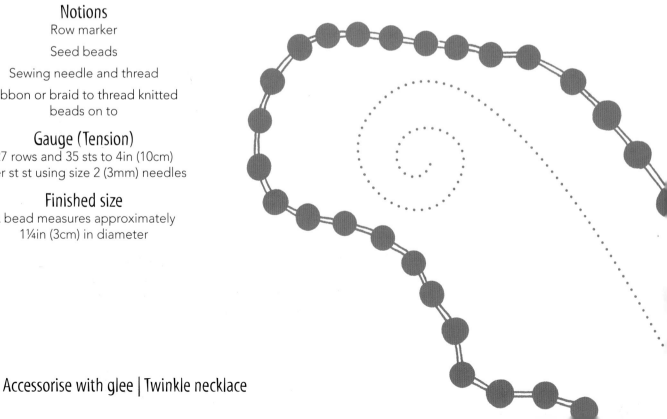

Knitting notes

You can embellish the knitted beads with seed beads, sequins or tiny buttons; whatever takes your fancy!

I used a 2-ply yarn doubled to knit the beads, but you can use a 4-ply yarn single instead. A smaller ball will still knit lots of beads.

The individual beads and the Button Necklace are knitted in the same way, you just finish off after every bobble for the beads and stuff them, while for the Button Necklace you keep going and then flatten the bobbles out to make discs.

Stitch 'n' smile

It goes without saying that you'll want accessories to match your outfits, and this pattern is so quick to do that you can spend an afternoon making the perfect necklace to wear that evening.

GET KNITTING

Cast on 6 sts using size 2 (3mm) needles.
Rnd 1 K6.
Work as i-cord as follows:
Slide sts to other end of needle without turning. Pull working yarn across the back of the i-cord.
Cont to work i-cord until the cord measures approx. 2in (5cm).

Stitch 'n' smile

This is a great stash buster project, and the results make an excellent gift. Using up stash and making people happy – knitting heaven!

BEAD

** **Next rnd** [Kfb] 6 times. (12 sts)
Divide sts equally over 3 needles.
Place marker to mark beg of round.
Next rnd K12.
With RS facing, keeping gauge (tension)
fairly tight on first rnd, work in the rnd
as follows:
Next rnd [K1, kfb] 6 times. (18 sts)
Next rnd K18.
Next rnd [K2, kfb] 6 times. (24 sts)
Next rnd K24.
Next rnd [K3, kfb] 6 times. (30 sts)
Next rnd K30.
Next rnd [K4, kfb] 6 times. (36 sts)
Next rnd K36.
Next rnd [K4, k2tog] 6 times. (30 sts)
Next rnd K30.
Next rnd [K3, k2tog] 6 times. (24 sts)
Next rnd K24.
Next rnd [K2, k2tog] 6 times. (18 sts)
Next rnd K18.
Next rnd [K1, k2tog] 6 times. (12 sts)
Next rnd K12.
Next rnd [K2tog] 6 times. (6 sts)**
Stuff the bead with spare yarn, cut working yarn
and thread end through rem 6 sts, pull up tight
and secure end of yarn.

Making up

Loop the end of the i-cord to join
the bead and sew in place. Sew seed
beads randomly over the surface.
Make as many knitted beads as
desired and thread onto ribbon or
braid to make necklace.

Button necklace

This version of the Twinkle Necklace is decorated with vintage and new buttons.

YOU WILL NEED

Yarn
1 x 3½oz (100g) ball fingering-weight (4-ply) yarn – minimum 318yds (293m) – this amount could make several necklaces, or one very long one!

Needles
4 x size 2 (3mm) double-pointed knitting needles

Notions
Row marker

Buttons of varying sizes from ¾in–1¼in (2–3cm) diameter

Sewing needle and thread

Gauge (Tension)
27 rows and 35 sts to 4in (10cm) over st st using size 2 (3mm) needles

Finished size
Up to you! A disc measures approximately 2in (5cm) when flattened out.

GET KNITTING

Cast on 6 sts using size 2 (3mm) needles.
Rnd 1 K6.
Work as i-cord as follows:
Slide sts to other end of needle without turning. Pull working yarn across the back of the i-cord.
***Cont to work i-cord until the cord measures approx. 4in (10cm). Cont work as for Beaded Beads from ** to **.
Slide all 6 sts onto one needle.
Next rnd K6.***
Rep from *** to *** until necklace is desired length.
Bind (cast) off.

Making up

Weave in loose ends.
Knot i-cord at various points if you wish and knot ends together. Flatten out the discs and sew a button to the centre of each one.

Pom-pom scarf

Here's a very simple to make version of the Twinkle Necklace that's a perfect project for children to tackle.

YOU WILL NEED

Yarn
1 x 4oz (100g) ball worsted-weight (Aran) yarn – minimum 210yds (193m)

Notions
2 x 3in (8cm) squares of thin card for templates

Scissors

Knitter's sewing needle

Finished size
39½in (1m) long

GET MAKING

Cut two 3in (8cm) circles from the card. Cut concentric 1½in (4cm) diameter circles in the centre of each. Hold the two circles together as one.

Wrap the yarn through the middle hole and around the outer circle. Continue to wrap the yarn until you have covered the card with several layers of yarn.

Wiggle the scissors in between the card circles and cut through the yarn that wraps them. Cut a length of yarn approximately 10in (25cm) long. Slide the length of yarn between the two card circles, pull tight and tie a very firm double knot to secure the bundle of cut yarn. Slide off the card circles.

Trim any stray ends to neaten the pom-pom, leaving long the tails of the yarn used to tie it.

Make as many pom-poms as you want, then join them together. Thread one tail into a knitter's sewing needle, thread it through the middle of the next pom-pom in the necklace, then back through the pom-pom it came from. Knot the two tails together and trim the ends. Repeat this with every pom-pom to complete the scarf.

Special instructions and tips
I found it easier to weigh out the yarn into ⅛oz (5g) balls – each ball making one pom-pom.

Feng Shui purse

A pretty coin purse that will make the most of your money, and its bigger sister for when you strike it rich. According to Feng Shui, the colour green represents growth and development, so a green purse will help to contribute positively to your financial situation.

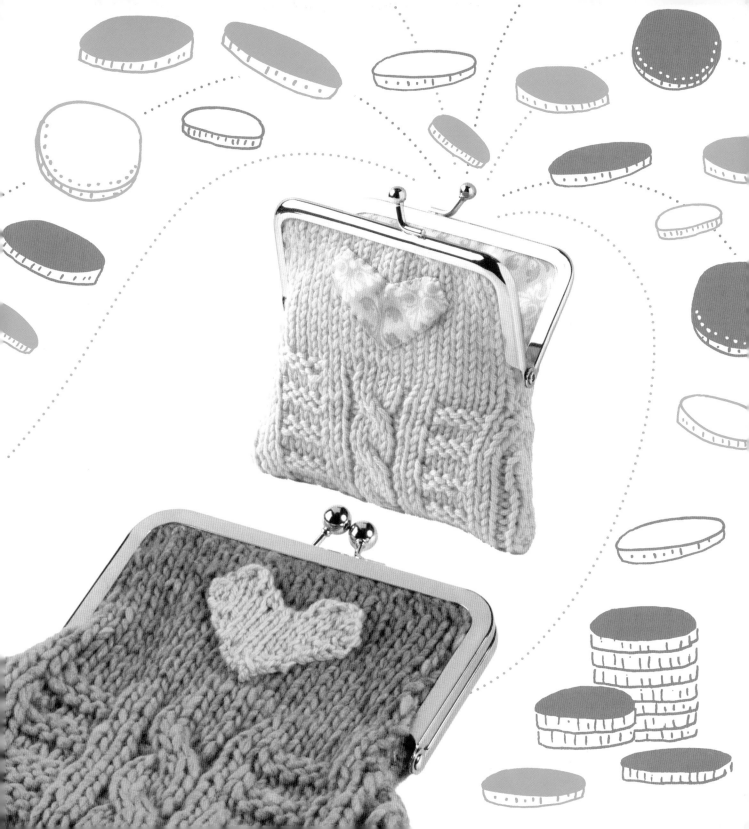

Coin purse

A little purse for your pocket.

YOU WILL NEED

Yarn
1 x 1¾oz (50g) ball sport-weight (DK) yarn – minimum 100yds (92m)

Needles
2 x size 6 (4mm) knitting needles

1 x size 6 (4mm) cable needle

Notions
12in (30cm) lightweight fabric for lining

Small-sized silver purse frame, approx. 4 x 2in (10 x 5cm)

Sewing needle and thread

Fabric glue

Gauge (Tension)
30 rows and 22 sts to 4in (10cm) over st st using sport-weight (DK) yarn and size 6 (4mm) needles

Finished size
Approx. 5in (13cm) wide at widest point x 4in (10cm) high

Happy yarn
The yarn used here is Rowan Belle Organic, which is a mix of 50% wool and 50% cotton. This makes it hardwearing as well as soft to the touch, perfect for a pocket purse.

Special instructions and tips
C4F – slip next 2 sts p-wise onto cable needle and hold at front of work, knit next 2 sts from left-hand needle, then knit 2 sts from cable needle.

Cable patt
Patt row 1 (RS) P1, k2, p4, k2, p1, k4, p1, k2, p4, k2, p1.
Patt row 2 K1, p2, k4, p2, k1, p4, k1, p2, k4, p2, k1.
Patt row 3 P1, k8, p1, k4, p1, k8, p1.
Patt row 4 K1, p8, k1, p4, k1, p8, k1.
Patt row 5 P1, k2, p4, k2, p1, C4F, p1, k2, p4, k2, p1.
Patt row 6 K1, p2, k4, p2, k1, p4, k1, p2, k4, p2, k1.
Patt row 7 P1, k8, p1, k4, p1, k8, p1.

Patt row 8 K1, p8, k1, p4, k1, p8, k1.
Patt row 9 P1, k2, p4, k2, p1, k4, p1, k2, p4, k2, p1.
Patt row 10 K1, p2, k4, p2, k1, p4, k1, p2, k4, p2, k1.
Patt row 11 P1, k8, p1, C4F, p1, k8, p1.
Patt row 12 K1, p8, k1, p4, k1, p8, k1.

These 12 rows form the cable pattern.

Knitting notes

Look out for other purse frames, either in craft stores or online. There are many types to choose from – traditional antique-style ones or more contemporary versions. Knit up a quick gauge (tension) square from the yarn you wish to use to work out the needle size needed to get the number of stitches written in the pattern to correspond with the width of the purse frame you have chosen.

If you are unsure about cabling you could knit the pattern without it; just knit or purl the rows instead of adding in the pattern.

Because you are only using one small ball of yarn, why not treat yourself to a luxurious and expensive yarn to make an extra-special purse for a lovely gift, or indeed for yourself?

Stitch 'n' smile

This is a very simple cable pattern, so don't be put off if you've not knitted cables before. Practise with some spare yarn before you start your purse to make sure you get the technique right.

GET KNITTING

Cast on 22 sts using size 6 (4mm) needles.
**Beg with a k row, work 15 rows st st.
Place marker at each end of next row to mark 'hinge point'.
Row 16 (WS) Pfkb, p20, pfkb. (24 sts)
Rows 17–18 Beg with *Patt Row 1*, patt 2 rows as set.
Row 19 Cast on 2 sts, k2, patt next 24 sts (*Patt Row 3*). (26 sts)
Row 20 Cast on 2 sts, p2, patt next 24 sts, p2. (28 sts)
Row 21 K2, patt next 24 sts, k2.
Row 22 P2, patt next 24 sts, p2.
Row 23 K2, patt next 24 sts, k2.
Cont to work patt as set, working 2 sts st st either side of 24 patt sts over next 22 rows.
Row 46 P2tog, patt next 24 sts as *Patt Row 6* – (k1, p2, k4, p2, k1, p4, k1, p2, k4, p2, k1), p2tog. (26 sts)
Row 47 Skpo, k8, p1, k4, p1, k8, k2tog. (24 sts)
Row 48 P2tog, p to last 2 sts, p2tog. (22 sts)
Cont in st st for 4 rows.

KNITTED-IN HEART MOTIF

Row 53 (RS) K10, p2, k to end.
Row 54 P9, k4, p to end.
Row 55 K8, p6, k to end.
Row 56 P8, k6, p to end.
Row 57 K7, p8, k to end.
Row 58 P6, k4, p2, k4, p to end.
Row 59 K6, p4, k2, p4, k to end.
Row 60 P7, k2, p4, k2, p to end.
Cont in st st for 3 rows.
Bind (cast) off.**

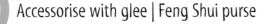

Heart embellishment

If you wish, use tracing paper to trace around the knitted heart, cut the heart out of paper and use it as a template to draw around onto the reverse side of the same fabric as used for the lining. Add a ¼in (6mm) seam allowance all around before cutting out the fabric heart. Press the seam allowance to the wrong side. Appliqué the fabric heart in place on the opposite side of the purse to the knitted-in heart.

Alternatively, work a simple running stitch around the knitted heart in a contrasting yarn.

Making up

Use the completed knitted panel as a template from which to cut the fabric lining, allowing at least ½in (1cm) all around for seams. Cut one piece of lining material.

Press seam allowance on the fabric lining panel to the wrong side (WS). Tack WS of lining panel to WS of knitted panel.

Using needle and sewing thread, sew fabric panel to knitted panel around the edges.

With knitted sides facing each other, fold the purse in half. Working a backstitch seam, sew both side seams from hinge point down to fold on both sides of purse.

Following manufacturer's instructions, apply glue generously to one side of purse frame and to top and side edges of fabric around one side of purse opening. Allow glue to dry for 5 minutes, or as recommended by manufacturer.

Insert one side of purse into frame, starting at hinge point and working around the top and down the other side. Check that the lining is also inserted evenly. Allow to dry for 15 minutes. Glue other side of the purse fabric into the frame in the same way.

Stitch 'n' smile
Choose a really pretty lining for your purse. It might not be on display, but it'll make you happy to know that the inside of your purse is as lovely as the outside.

Big purse

Add a touch of wealth-attracting green to this purse with a lime-coloured heart motif.

YOU WILL NEED

Yarn

1 x 1¾oz (50g) ball bulky-weight (chunky) yarn – minimum 100yds (92m)

Small amount of lime-green worsted-weight (Aran) yarn

Needles

2 x size 10½ (7mm) needles

1 x size 10½ (7mm) cable needle

2 x size 8 (5mm) needles

Notions

24in (60cm) lightweight fabric for lining

Medium-sized silver purse frame, approx. 6 x 3in (15 x 8cm)

Sewing needle and thread

Fabric glue

Gauge (Tension)

18 rows and 14 sts to 4in (10cm), using bulky-weight (chunky) yarn and size 10½ (7mm) needles

Finished size

Approx. 8in (20cm) wide at widest point x 7in (18cm) high

Happy yarn

Pick a pinstripe or Harris tweed-effect yarn to suit your suit – or maybe a linen yarn or a special silk to make your purse even more desirable.

GET KNITTING

Cast on 22 sts using size 10½ (7mm) needles. Work as for Coin Purse from ** to **.

Heart patch

Using worsted-weight (Aran) yarn and size 8 (5mm) knitting needles, put slip knot loosely on needle, kfb into slip knot, then before slipping the new stitch off the needle, knit the stitch again. (3 sts)

Row 1 P.
Row 2 Kfb, k1, kfb. (5 sts)
Row 3 P.
Row 4 Kfb, k3, kfb. (7 sts)
Row 5 P.
Row 6 Kfb, k5, kfb. (9 sts)
Row 7 P.
Row 8 Kfb, k7, kfb. (11 sts)
Row 9 P.
Row 10 Kfb, k4, bind (cast) off 1 st, one st on needle k3, kfb. (12 sts)
Row 11 P6, turn.
Row 12 *K2tog, k2, k2tog, turn.
Row 13 P.
Row 14 [K2tog] twice. (2 sts)
Break yarn, thread end through rem 2 sts. Fasten off.**
WS facing, rejoin yarn to rem 6 sts.
Row 11 P.
Rep from * to **.
Weave in all ends and, if necessary, press heart motif flat.
Sew the motif onto the purse opposite the knitted-in heart.
Make up as for Coin Purse.

Stitch 'n' smile

Go for party appeal by knitting a purse to use as an on-trend clutch bag, just big enough to hold your lipstick, phone, house keys and money. Add a silky lining for extra glamour.

Hug a mug cosy

RATING   Fast-track fun

Delicious hot chocolate? Energy-boosting coffee? Relaxing tea? Whatever your preferred take-away drink, you need a cosy to keep it warm, and to stop the beaker burning you. Keep a cosy in your handbag for your on-the-way-to-the-office drink. For times when you have a proper china mug to drink from, there's a button-up version to fit your favourite cup.

Take-away cup cosies

I ♡ coffee, I ♡ tea and I (absolutely and guiltily) ♡ hot chocolate take-away cup cosies!

YOU WILL NEED

Yarn
1 x 1¾oz (50g) ball bulky-weight (chunky) yarn – minimum 103yds (95m): this amount makes four mug cosies

Needles
4 x size 8 (5mm) double-pointed knitting needles

Notions
Knitter's sewing needle

Gauge (Tension)
19 rows and 15 sts to 4in (10cm) over st st using size 8 (5mm) needles

Finished size
To fit both 12oz take-away cup approx, 3½in (9cm) diameter x 4¼in (10.5cm) tall; and 16oz take-away cups, approx: 4in (10cm) diameter x 4¾in (12cm) tall

Happy yarn
Make a practical yarn choice (as well as a pretty one) by making sure that your yarn is washable. No-one loves a grubby cup cosy!

Knitting notes

Instead or a heart motif you could use the same technique to work your initials into a cup cosy. Using graph paper (every square representing a knitted stitch), draw out the letter you want by putting a cross in each appropriate square. On right-side rows of the knitting, work a purl stitch for every cross and on wrong side rows, work a knit stitch.

Stitch 'n' smile

I've chosen yarn colours to complement the hot drinks, but you could match your cosy to your coat, or knit a scarf and matching cosy for really coordinated winter style.

GET KNITTING

16oz cup

Cast on 24 sts using size 8 (5mm) needles.

**WS facing, slip 24 sts p-wise and divide equally over three needles. With RS facing, keeping gauge (tension) fairly tight on first rnd, work in the rnd as follows:

Rnd 1 K.

Place marker to mark beg of rnd. Rep last rnd twice more.

Rnd 4 [Kfb, k11] twice. (26 sts)
Rnd 5 [K7, p1, k5] twice.
Rnd 6 [K6, p3, k4] twice.
Rnd 7 [K5, p2, k1, p2, k3] twice.
Rnd 8 [K4, p2, k3, p2, k2] twice.
Rnd 9 Kfb, k2, p2, k5, p2, k1, kfb, k2, p2, k5, p2, k1. (28 sts)
Rnd 10 [K3, p2, k7, p2] twice.
Rnd 11 [K3, p2, k3, p1, k3, p2] twice.
Rnd 12 [K3, p2, k2, p3, k2, p2] twice.
Rnd 13 [K4, p4, k1, p4, k1] twice.

Rnd 14 Kfb, k4, p2, k3, p2, k2, kfb, k4, p2, k3, p2, k2. (30 sts)
Rnd 15 K.

Rep last rnd once.**

Rnd 17 [K9, p1, k5] twice.
Rnd 18 [K8, p3, k4] twice.
Rnd 19 Kfb, k6, p2, k1, p2, k3, kfb, k6, p2, k1, p2, k3. (32 sts)
Rnd 20 [K7, p2, k3, p2, k2] twice.
Rnd 21 [K6, p2, k5, p2, k1] twice.
Rnd 22 [K5, p2, k7, p2] twice.
Rnd 23 [K5, p2, k3, p1, k3, p2] twice.
Rnd 24 Kfb, k4, p2, k2, p3, k2, p2, kfb, k4, p2, k2, p3, k2, p2. (34 sts)
Rnd 25 [K7, p4, k1, p4, k1] twice.
Rnd 26 [K8, p2, k3, p2, k2] twice.
Rnd 27 K.

Rep last rnd once more.

Rnd 29 [Kfb, k16] twice. (36 sts)
Rnd 29 K.

Bind (cast) off.

12oz cup

Cast on 24 sts using size 8
(5mm) needles.
Work as 16oz Cup from ** to **.
(30 sts)
Rnds 17–18 K.
Bind (cast) off.

Making up

Weave in ends.

Mug cosy

Make cosies to match the colours of your mugs at home and in the office.

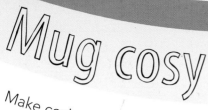

YOU WILL NEED

Yarn
1 x 1¾oz (50g) ball worsted-weight (Aran) yarn – minimum 87yds (80m): this amount makes three mug cosies

Needles
2 x size 8 (5mm) knitting needles

Notions
2 x buttons approx. ½in (11mm) diameter

Knitter's sewing needle

Sewing needle and thread

Gauge (Tension)
20 rows and 17 sts to 4in (10cm) over st st using size 8 (5mm) needles

Finished size
To fit average coffee mug with handle: my mug is 10¼in (26cm) in circumference.

Happy yarn
Tweed yarns give lovely, subtle colour variations to your knitting all by themselves; no extra work needed from you!

Special instructions and tips
Backward Loop Cast On is the best cast-on method when adding stitches in the middle of a row, as for the buttonhole in this pattern.

GET KNITTING
Cast on 14 sts using size 8 (5mm) needles.
Row 1 Sl1, k.
Row 2 Sl1, p.
Rep last 2 rows 23 times, or until piece measures 9½in (24cm), ending with a WS row.

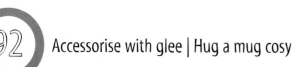

Knitting notes

A lovely gift would be a mug, mug cosy and a packet of specialist coffee or fine tea.

If you have a specific mug in mind to use with this cosy, you can make the cosy to fit by adding or taking away rows before the Buttonhole Strap instruction.

Stitch 'n' smile

Choose a really cute button for your cosy. There are lots of fun ones that'll make you smile every time you sip.

BUTTONHOLE STRAP

Row 49 (RS) Bind (cast) off 2 sts, k to end. (12 sts)
Row 50 Bind (cast) off 2 sts, p to end. (10 sts)
Row 51 Sl1, k9.
Row 52 Sl1, p9.
Rep last 2 rows 3 times more.

BUTTONHOLE

Row 59 Sl1, k2, [k2tog] twice, k3. (8 sts)
Row 60 Sl1, p3, cast on 2 sts, p4. (10 sts)
Row 61 K2tog, k6, k2tog. (8 sts)
Row 62 P2tog, p4, p2tog. (6 sts)
Row 63 K2tog, k2, k2tog. (4 sts)
Row 64 [P2tog] twice. (2 sts)
Row 65 [K2tog]. (1 st)
Fasten off.

Making up

Weave in ends. Wrap the cosy around the mug you wish to keep warm. Place a pin at the place where you want the button to be, to correspond with the buttonhole. Sew on the button. If you wish, sew another button, about an 1in (2.5cm) away from the first button so that the cosy can be adjusted to fit a wider mug (as shown).

Monster happy

A feel-good challenge

A mini monster, a medium monster and a monster-sized monster, but not the kind to give you bad dreams – these quirky guys are cuddly and silly, and are more likely to make you giggle than make you scream. But give them a name otherwise they may turn nasty! Mine are called Scary Custard, Purple People Eater (actually he prefers toast) and Terrible Blue Creature. Try making Terrible Blue first – he's the smallest – then experiment with the others.

Mini monster

A cute little chap to start you on the monster trail.

YOU WILL NEED

Yarn
1 x 1¾oz (50g) ball fingering-weight (4-ply) yarn – minimum 164yds (150m)

Needles
4 x size 3 (3.25mm) double-pointed knitting needles

Notions
1, 2 or 3 odd-sized buttons for eyes, plus 1 with which to sew on the tail

Sewing needle and black and white sewing thread

Stitch holders (optional)

Toy filling

Gauge (Tension)
38 rows and 28 sts to 4in (10cm) using over st st using size 3 (3.25mm) needles

Finished size
Approx. 10¼in (26cm) tall x 7½in (19cm) wide (arms outstretched)

Happy yarn
Lovely soft merino yarn makes for a deliciously huggable monster.

Special instructions and tips
Stuff the head, arms and legs fairly firmly but leave the body a little floppier to give your monster cuddle factor.

Knitting notes

Rather than use a stitch holder, when I need to hold stitches that are not in use while knitting in the round I find it easier to thread the stitches onto a spare length of yarn, preferably a thicker yarn than the yarn I'm knitting with.

To avoid gaps between the junctions (called 'ladders') when going from one needle to the next while knitting in the round, try knitting the first and second stitches on the new needle then giving the working yarn a little tug to keep it snug to the needle.

The monsters' heads are all interchangeable, whether you knit the mini, medium or monster monster. Also, why not design your own? It is just a simple case of increasing (M1) and/or decreasing (k2tog or skpo) where you want shape.

Stitch 'n' smile
Colour really changes the look of these monsters. Try them in pastels for cute toys to make a baby chuckle.

GET KNITTING

Legs

FIRST LEG

Cast on 18 sts using size 3 (3.25mm) needles.
***Slip 18 sts p-wise and divide them equally over 3 needles.
With RS facing, keeping gauge (tension) fairly tight on first rnd, work in the rnd as follows:
Rnd 1 K18.
Place marker to mark beg of rnd.
Rep last rnd 16 times more.
Rnd 18 Cast on 10 sts, k28.
Turn with WS facing.
Row 19 (WS) Cast on 10 sts, p38.
Break yarn, leave sts on a length of spare yarn (or stitch holder).

OTHER LEG

Cast on 18 sts using size 3 (3.25mm) needles.
Slip 18 sts p-wise and divide them equally over 3 needles.
With RS facing, keeping gauge (tension) fairly tight on first rnd, work in the rnd as follows:
Rnd 1 K18.
Place marker. Rep last rnd 18 times more.

JOIN BOTH LEGS

Rnd 20 K next 9 sts onto one needle. Slip next 9 sts onto the needle behind, giving 9 sts on n1 and 9 sts on n2.
Slip 38 sts held on spare yarn (or stitch holder) p-wise and divide evenly over the other 2 needles.
Cont rnd 20, knit across these 38 sts, then across next 9 sts from second leg. Join in rnd. (56 sts)
On this last rnd, take care not to twist the stitches and keep gauge (tension) fairly tight.
At this point you may wish to redistribute the sts more evenly over the needles.
Rnd 21 K56.
Place marker.
Rep last rnd 33 times more.
Rnd 55 K28, turn.
With WS facing, work back and forth as follows:

DIVIDE FOR FRONT AND ARMHOLES

Row 56 P28.
Row 57 Sl1, skpo, k to last 3 sts, k2tog, k1. (26 sts)
Row 58 P.
Rep last 2 rows 4 times more. (18 sts)
Cut yarn, slip sts off needle onto a length of spare yarn (or stitch holder).

Back

Row 55 (RS) Rejoin yarn to 28 sts for Back and knit across.
Row 56 P.
Row 57 Sl1, skpo, k to last 3 sts, k2tog, k1. (26 sts)
Row 58 P.
Rep last 2 rows 4 times more. (18 sts)
Cut yarn, slip sts off needle onto a length of spare yarn (or stitch holder).

Arms

Using size 3 (3.25mm) needles, RS facing, rejoin yarn at shoulder where you divided for Front and Back, pick up and k18 sts along row ends of armholes.
Next row P18.
Divide sts over 3 needles: 6 sts on n1, 6 sts on n2, 6 sts on n3.
With RS facing, keeping gauge (tension) fairly tight on first rnd, work in the rnd as follows:
Place marker to mark beg of rnd.
Rnd 1 K18.
Rep last rnd 25 times more.
Bind (cast) off. **
Rep from ** to ** for other arm.

Neck

With RS facing, sl 36 sts p-wise from the spare yarn (or stitch holders) for the neck equally onto 2 size 3 (3.25mm) needles.
Rejoin yarn, divide sts over 3 needles: 12 sts on n1, 12 sts on n2, 12 sts on n3.
With RS facing, keeping gauge (tension) fairly tight on first rnd, work in the rnd as follows:
Rnd 67 K17, k2tog, k16, skpo (taking one st from next rnd). (34 sts).
Pull yarn tight as you knit across the junctions between needles.
Rnd 68 K34.
Rep last rnd twice more.

SHAPE NECK

Rnd 71 M1, k17, M1, k17. (36 sts)
Rnd 72 K36.
Rnd 73 M1, k18, M1, k18. (38 sts)
Rnd 74 K38.
Rnd 75 M1, k19, M1, k19. (40 sts)
Rnd 76 K40.
Rnd 77 M1, k20, M1, k20. (42 sts)
Rnd 78 K42.
Rnd 79 M1, k21, M1, k21. (44 sts)
Rnd 80 K44.
Rnd 81 M1, k22, M1, k22. (46 sts)
Rnd 82 K46.***
Rep last rnd once more.

SHAPE HEAD

Rnd 84 K1, M1, k21, M1, [k1, M1] twice, k21, M1, k1, M1. (52 sts)

Rnd 85 [K1, M1] 3 times, k18, [M1, k1] 7 times, k21, [M1, k1] 3 times, M1. (66 sts)

Rnd 86 [K1, M1] 5 times, k23, [M1, k1] 11 times, k22, [M1, k1] 5 times, M1. (88 sts)

Rnd 87 K88.

Rep last rnd twice more.

Rnd 90 K42, k2tog, k42, skpo. (86 sts)

Rnd 91 K86.

Rnd 92 K39, k2tog, skpo, k39, k2tog, skpo. (82 sts)

Rnd 93 K82.

Rnd 94 K37, k2tog, skpo, k37, k2tog, skpo. (78 sts)

Rnd 95 K78.

Rnd 96 K35, k2tog, skpo, k35, k2tog, skpo. (74 sts)

Rnd 97 K33, k2tog, skpo, k33, k2tog, skpo. (70 sts)

Rnd 98 K31, k2tog, skpo, k31, k2tog, skpo. (66 sts)

Rnd 99 K29, k2tog, skpo, k29, k2tog, skpo. (62 sts)

Rnd 100 K27, k2tog, skpo, k27, k2tog, skpo. (58 sts)

SHAPE TOP OF HEAD

Rnd 101 Skpo, k25, k2tog, turn. (27 sts)

With WS facing, work back and forth as follows:

HEAD FRONT

Row 102 **P2tog, p23, p2tog. (25 sts)

Row 103 Skpo, k to last 2 sts from Head Front, k2tog. (23 sts)

Row 104 P2tog, p to last 2 sts from Head Front, p2tog. (21 sts)

Row 105 Skpo, k2tog, k to last 4 sts from Head Front, k2tog, skpo. (17 sts)

Row 106 [P2tog] twice, p to last 4 sts from Head Front, [p2tog] twice. (13 sts)

Bind (cast) off. **

HEAD BACK

Row 101 (RS) Rejoin yarn, skpo, k to last 2 sts, k2tog. (27 sts)

Shape Head Back as Head Front from ** to **.

Spikes

Using double thickness yarn and size 3 (3.25mm) needles, [cast on 6 sts, bind (cast) off 6 sts] 12 times. Bind (cast) off.

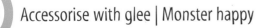

Stitch 'n' smile

You could use a fluffy yarn or a novelty eyelash yarn to turn this monster's spikes into mad punky hair. You might need to double the yarn again to make it thick enough.

Tail

Cast on 6 sts using double thickness yarn and size 3 (3.25mm) needles.
Row 1 K6.
Work as i-cord as follows:
Slide sts to other end of needle without turning.
Pull working yarn across the back of the knitting.
Cont to work i-cord until the tie measures approx. 2in (5cm).
Next row [K2tog] 3 times. (3 sts)
Cut yarn and thread end through sts.
Pull up tight and secure.

Making up

Sew the eyes onto head front. Embroider a straight stitch mouth and triangular teeth in black thread, fill in teeth with white thread, or make up your own face. Turn body out to WS. Slip the row of spikes in between the head seam edges with the spikes sandwiched between the front and back of head, the straight edge aligning with the bound (cast) off edges of head. Join head back to head front and row of spikes together.
Join the bound (cast) off ends at hands, you may need to work a few stitches to close any gaps at the shoulders. Join feet. Turn out to RS.
Sew a button to the top of the tail at cast on end then sew the tail to the middle body back, just above the legs.
Stuff the arms, legs, body, head and ears. Close the gap between the legs using mattress stitch, working the seam into the knitting about ¼in (6mm) up from the cast on edges to compensate for the 'stepping' caused by the cast on edges.
To complete and give shape to the feet, pinch the back of the foot to create a 'heel' sew the 'pinched' bit of knitting in place with a couple of stitches.

Medium monster

A spiky collar makes this guy a monster with style.

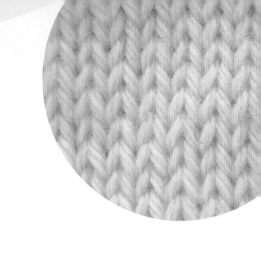

YOU WILL NEED

Yarn
1 x 3½oz (100g) ball/skein worsted-weight (Aran) yarn – minimum 164yds (150m)

Needles
4 x size 5 (3.75mm) double-pointed knitting needles

Notions
1, 2 or 3 odd sized buttons for eyes, plus 1 with which to sew on the tail

Sewing needle and black and white sewing thread

Stitch holders (optional)

Toy filling

Gauge (Tension)
25 rows and 21 sts to 4in (10cm) over st st using size 5 (3.75mm) needles

Finished size
Approx. 14½in (37cm) tall x 12in (30cm) wide (arms outstretched)

Happy yarn
The yarn used here is Cascade 220, which comes in a monstrously huge range of colours so there's bound to be one you love.

GET KNITTING

Cast on 18 sts using size 5 (3.75mm) needles.
Cont to work as Mini Monster from *** to ***.

SHAPE HEAD

Rnd 83 M1, k23, M1, k23. (48 sts)
Rnd 84 K48.
Rnd 85 M1, k24, M1, k24. (50 sts)
Rnd 86 K50.
Rnd 87 M1, k25, M1, k25. (52 sts)
Rnd 88 K52.****
Rnd 89 Bind (cast) off 8 sts, one st on needle k9, bind (cast) off 16 sts, one st on needle k9, bind (cast) off 8 sts. (20 sts)

Rnd 90 Rejoin yarn and divide sts: K7 on n1, k6 sts on n2, k7 sts on n3. With RS facing, keeping gauge (tension) fairly tight on first rnd, with n4 work in the rnd as follows: Place marker to mark beg of rnd.
Rnd 91 K20.
Rep last rnd 10 times more.
Rnd 102 [K2tog] 10 times. (10 sts).
Rnd 103 [K2tog] 5 times. (5 sts).
Cut yarn and thread end through sts, pull up tight and secure.

Tail

Cast on 6 sts using size 5 (3.75mm) needles.
Work tail as for Mini Monster.

Collar

Cast on 3 sts using size 5 (3.75mm) needles.
Foundation row K2, yo, k1. (4 sts)
Patt rows
Row 1 K.
Row 2 K2, yo, k2. (5 sts)
Row 3 K.
Row 4 K2, yo, k3. (6 sts)
Row 5 K.

Row 6 K2, yo, k4. (7 sts)
Row 7 K.
Row 8 Bind (cast) off 6 sts. (1 st)
Row 9 One st on needle, cast on 2 sts, k2, yo, k1. (4 sts)
Rep last 9 patt rows 5 times more, leaving out row 9 on last triangle. (6 triangles made) (1 st)
Fasten off.

Making up

Sew the eyes onto head front. Embroider a straight stitch mouth and triangular teeth in black thread, fill in teeth with white thread, or make up your own face. RS facing, join top of head with mattress stitch.
Turn body out to WS. Join the bound (cast) off ends at hands, you may need to work a few stitches to close any gaps at the shoulders. Join feet. Turn to RS. Sew a button to the top of the tail at cast on end then sew the tail to the middle body back, just above the legs.
Stuff the arms, legs, body, head and ears. Close the gap between the legs with mattress seam, working the seam into the knitting about ¼in (6mm) up from the cast on edges to compensate for the 'stepping' caused by the cast on edges.
Sew on the collar around the neck. To complete and give shape to the feet, pinch the back of the foot to create a 'heel', sew the 'pinched' bit of knitting in place with a couple of stitches.

Stitch 'n' smile

You can give your monster unique personality by the way you embroider his face. Great big teeth or fluttering stitched eyelashes, a huge grin or pom-pom nose are all good to try.

Monster monster

The row of spikes on this big boy would make him scary, if he wasn't as soft as a kitten!

YOU WILL NEED

Yarn
1 x 3½oz (100g) ball/skein worsted-weight (Aran) yarn – minimum 164yds (150m)

Needles
4 x size 8 (5mm) double-pointed knitting needles

Notions
1, 2 or 3 odd sized buttons for eyes

Sewing needle and black and white sewing thread

Stitch holders (optional)

Toy filling

Gauge (Tension)
24 rows and 18 sts to 4in (10cm) using size 8 (5mm) needles

Finished size
Approx. 16½in tall (41cm) x 12¾in (32cm) wide (arms outstretched)

Happy yarn
Self-striping yarn is a great (and very easy) way to add extra pizzazz to your monster.

GET KNITTING

Cast on 18 sts using size 8 (5mm) needles.
Cont to work as Medium Monster from ******* to ********. (52 sts)
Rnd 89 K25, k2tog, k24, borrowing 1 stitch from next rnd, skpo. (50 sts)
Rnd 90 K50.
Rnd 91 K23, k2tog, k23, skpo. (48 sts)
Row 92 K48.
Rnd 93 K6, bind (cast) off 12 sts, one st on needle k11, bind (cast) off 12 sts, one st on needle k5. (24 sts)

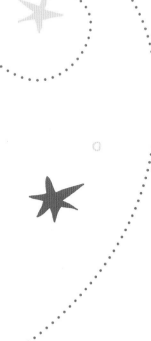

Accessorise with glee | Monster happy

SHAPE HORNS

Rnd 94 K6, slip next 12 sts onto spare yarn (stitch holder), k last 6 sts. (12 sts) Divide sts equally over 3 needles, join in rnd.

Rnd 95 K12.

Rep last rnd 7 times more.

Cut yarn and thread end through sts. Pull up tight and secure.

Rejoin yarn.

Slip 12 sts, held on spare yarn (or stitch holder), p-wise and divide evenly over 3 needles.

Rnd 94 K12.

Rep last rnd 8 times more.

Cut yarn and thread end through sts. Pull up tight and secure.

Stitch 'n' smile

If this monster isn't intended for a small child, you can add extra fun by knitting the horns longer and pushing pipecleaners inside them so that you can bend and shape them.

Spiky plates

Make as Collar on Medium Monster, rep patt 7 times and end as before. (8 triangles made)

Making up

Make up as for Medium Monster, sewing the spiky plates down the monster's back and along the tail. No need to sew a button on this monster's tail.

TECHNIQUES

ABBREVIATIONS

All knitting patterns use abbreviations to save time and space. These may seem a bit daunting if you are not familiar with the terms, but you will quickly pick up the language. Below is a list of all the abbreviations used in the patterns in this book.

The rows and rounds in the patterns in this book are numbered sequentially throughout each project piece so that you can easily identify where you are in the pattern.

approx approximately
beg beginning
cm(s) centimetre(s)
cont continue
dec decrease
DK double knitting
g gram(s)
in(s) inch(es)
inc increase
k knit
k2tog knit the next two stitches together (decrease by one stitch)
k3tog knit the next three stitches together (decrease by two stitches)
kfb knit into front and back of the same stitch (increase by one stitch)
mm millimetre(s)
M1 make one stitch
n needle (with the needle number: n1, n2, etc.)
oz ounce(s)
p purl
p2tog purl the next two stitches together (decrease by one stitch)

p3tog purl the next three stitches together (decrease by two stitches)
patt pattern
pfkb purl into front and knit into back of the same stitch (increase one stitch)
rem remaining
rep repeat
rnd round
RS right side
skpo slip one, knit one, pass the slipped stitch over (decrease by one stitch)
sl slip
sl1 slip one stitch
st(s) stitch(es)
st st stockinette stitch (stocking stitch)
tog together
WS wrong side
yo yarn over (increase by one stitch in lace pattern)
[ ] work instructions in square brackets as many times as directed
* work instructions between/after asterisks as directed

BASIC EQUIPMENT

You will, of course, need a selection of knitting needles. Some of the patterns use double-ended needles, but many use single-ended ones. You will also need a selection of safety pins and stitch holders for holding stitches, and markers to indicate the start of rounds. A large-eyed knitter's sewing needle will be handy for sewing up your projects.

GAUGE (TENSION)

On the band or sleeve of every ball of yarn there is information on the gauge (what European knitters call 'tension') of the yarn. This tells you how many stitches and rows you should aim to achieve over 4in (10cm) square. The gauge will differ depending on the size of the needles you use and the thickness of the yarn.

However, we all knit differently. Some people are naturally loose knitters and others knit more tightly. Knit a test swatch before starting a project and if your gauge doesn't match the instructions, then don't try to knit differently – everyone has a 'natural' gauge and you won't be able to keep up an 'unnatural' one. Instead, change the size of your knitting needles. If your gauge is too loose, then knit another swatch using needles a size smaller. If it's too tight, use needles a size larger. This might sound time-consuming, but it's quicker than knitting a whole project and finding that it doesn't fit.

CASTING ON

All projects start with getting the first stitches onto the
knitting needles – in other words, casting them on.

Knitting-on or lace cast on

There are various methods of casting on, but I find the knitting-on method
is simple and versatile. Of course, if you have a favourite method, do use that.

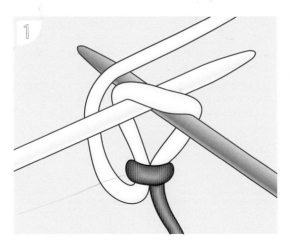

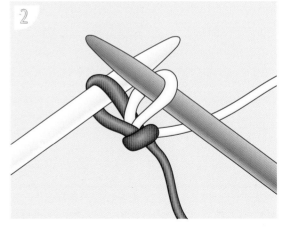

1 Make a slip knot in the working end of
your yarn, leaving an end of about 12in
(30cm). Place the slipknot on the left-hand
needle. Insert the right-hand needle into the
loop of the slip knot and wrap the yarn around
the tip of the needle, from back to front.

2 Slide the tip of the right-hand needle
down to catch this new loop of yarn and
draw it through the slip knot.

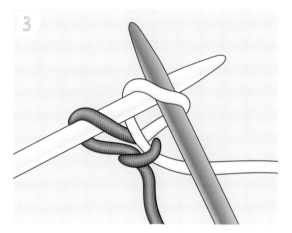

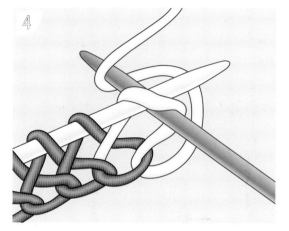

3 Place the new loop on the left-hand needle.

4 Repeat this process until you have cast on as many stitches as the project requires.

Backward loop cast on

This is the best cast-on method when adding stitches in the middle of a row.

Hold the working yarn in your left hand with the needle in your right. Extend your left index finger parallel to the yarn, dip your finger under the yarn and towards you. Slip the tip of the needle from left to right under the yarn around your finger, so that the needle is going through the loop in the same direction as your finger. Remove your finger, tighten the loop on the needle. You can see here how the yarn is twisted to make the loop lie on the needle in the correct direction.

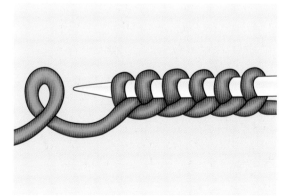

THE KNIT STITCH

The most basic stitch in knitting is called, not surprisingly, the knit stitch. It can be used completely on its own when knitting in the round to produce stockinette (stocking) stitch. When it is used on its own for working back and forth along rows, it produces garter stitch.

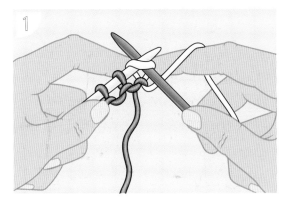

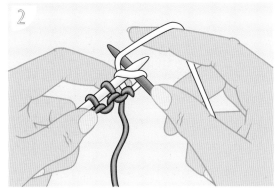

1 The working stitches will be on the left-hand needle. Take the right-hand needle and insert the tip from left to right into the first loop on the left-hand needle.

2 Wrap the yarn from back to front around the tip of the right-hand needle.

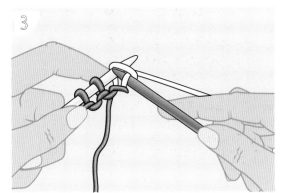

3 Slide the needle down to catch this new loop of yarn and draw it through the original loop on the left-hand needle. Slip the original loop off the left-hand needle, leaving the new loop on the right-hand needle. This is your first stitch. Repeat the process until all the stitches have been knitted off the left-hand needle onto the right-hand one.

THE PURL STITCH

The perfect complement to the knit stitch is the purl stitch. The right side of each looks like the reverse side of the other. If purl stitch is used when working back and forth, alternating rows with knit stitch, the combination produces stockinette (stocking) stitch.

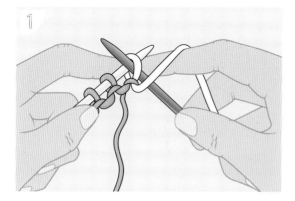

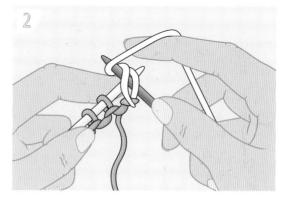

1 The working stitches will be on the left-hand needle. Take the right-hand needle and insert the tip from right to left into the first loop on the left-hand needle.

2 Wrap the yarn counterclockwise around the tip of the right-hand needle.

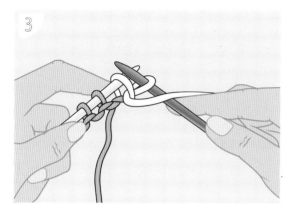

3 Use the tip of the right-hand needle to draw the new loop of yarn through the original loop on the left-hand needle. Slip the original loop off the left-hand needle, leaving the new loop on the right-hand needle. This is your first stitch. Repeat the process until all the stitches have been purled off the left-hand needle onto the right-hand one.

THE KNIT STITCH CONTINENTAL

In this method the yarn is held in the left hand. The right-hand needle moves to catch the yarn, which is held at the back of the work and is controlled by the left index finger.

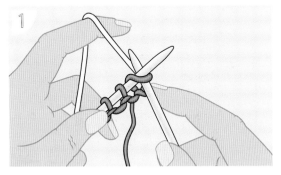

1 The working stitches will be on the left-hand needle and the yarn over your left index finger. Take the right-hand needle and insert the tip from left to right into the first loop on the left-hand needle.

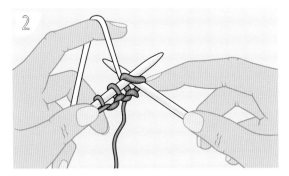

2 Move the right-hand needle down and across the back of the yarn.

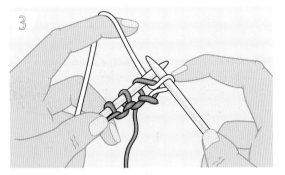

3 Draw the loop of yarn caught by the right-hand needle through the original loop on the left-hand needle. If need be, use your right index finger to hold the loop on the needle.

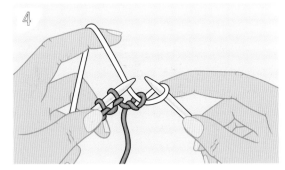

4 Slip the original loop off the left-hand needle and the new loop onto the right-hand needle. This is your first stitch. Repeat until all the stitches have been knitted off the left-hand needle onto the right-hand one.

THE PURL STITCH CONTINENTAL

Again, the yarn is held in the left hand, but in front of the work.

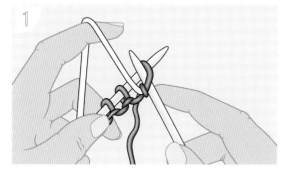

1 The working stitches will be on the left-hand needle and the yarn over your left index finger. Take the right-hand needle and insert the tip from right to left into the first loop on the left-hand needle.

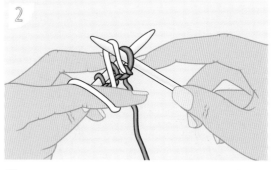

2 Move the right-hand needle from right to left behind the yarn and then from left to right in front of the yarn to hook a loop around this needle. Move your left index finger down in front of the work to keep the yarn tight.

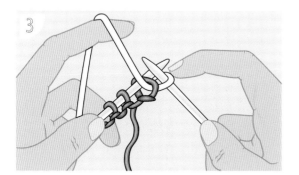

3 Draw the loop of yarn caught by the right-hand needle through the original loop on the left-hand needle. If need be, use your right index finger to hold the loop on the needle.

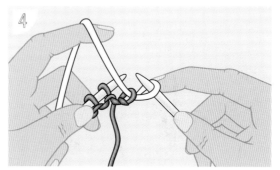

4 Slip the original loop off the left-hand needle and the new loop onto the right-hand needle. This is your first stitch. Move the left index finger back up to make the next stitch. Repeat until all the stitches have been purled off the left-hand needle onto the right-hand one.

BINDING (CASTING) OFF

To finish your projects you will need to bind (cast) off your knitting so that the stitches don't work loose.

Standard bind (cast) off

Here are instructions for binding (casting) off of one edge.

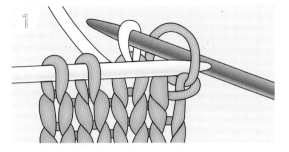 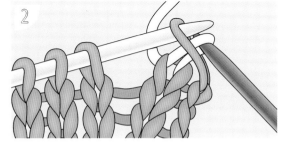

1 Knit the first two stitches on the left-hand needle in the usual way. Insert the left-hand needle into the first stitch on the right-hand needle.

2 Lift this stitch over the second stitch and drop it off the needle. This is the first bound (cast) off stitch. Knit the next stitch. Pass the new first stitch over the second stitch and drop it off the needle. Carry on until all the stitches have been bound (cast) off.

Kitchener stitch

This form of binding (casting) off is used to seamlessly join two pieces of knitting.

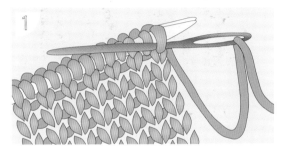

1 Cut the working yarn, leaving a long end, and thread it into a knitter's sewing needle. Hold the knitting needles, each with the same number of stitches on, parallel in your left hand. Insert the knitter's sewing needle purl-wise into the first stitch on the closest knitting needle. Pull the yarn through, leaving the stitch on the knitting needle.

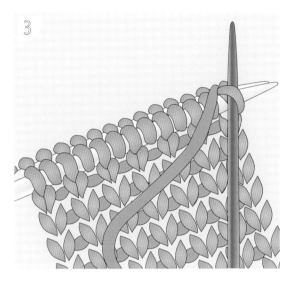

2 Insert the sewing needle knit-wise into the first stitch on the back knitting needle. Pull the yarn through, leaving the stitch on the needle.

3 Insert the sewing needle k-wise into the same front stitch as before, slip that stitch off the knitting needle onto the working yarn.

4 Insert the sewing needle p-wise into the next front stitch, leaving it on the knitting needle. Pass the sewing needle p-wise through the same stitch as before on the back knitting needle, slipping it off the needle. Insert the sewing needle k-wise through the next back stitch, leaving it on the knitting needle. Repeat Steps 3–4 until there are no stitches on the needles.

CABLING

This involves crossing a stitch or a group of stitches in front or behind each other using a separate, smaller, double-pointed needle called a cable needle.

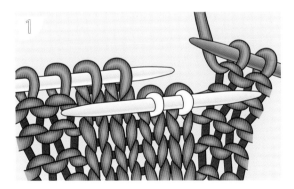

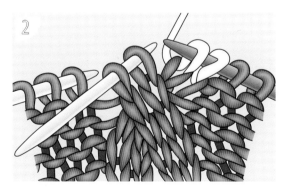

1 Work to where the cable will be. Slip the next 2 stitches p-wise onto the cable needle and hold it at the front of the work.

2 Knit the next 2 stitches, then knit 2 stitches from the cable needle. Hold the cable needle at the back to change cable direction.

SHAPING

Some projects have been created by shaping the knitting (increasing and decreasing stitches), as well as by knitting in the round and with the i-cord technique. The different shaping techniques you will need are explained here.

Decreasing stitches

Decreasing stitches is where you lose stitches, in these patterns usually one at a time. This can be achieved in several ways.

SKPO (SLIP ONE, KNIT ONE, PASS THE SLIPPED STITCH OVER)

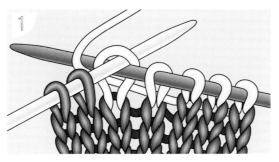

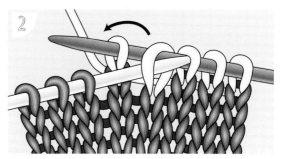

1 Knit along the row until you reach the area you want to decrease. Slip the stitch (un-knitted) onto the right-hand needle. Knit the next stitch.

2 Lift the slipped stitch over the knitted stitch and off the needle. This decreases by one stitch.

K2TOG (KNIT TWO STITCHES TOGETHER)

Knit along the row until you reach the area you want to decrease. Knit through the next two stitches as though they were one stitch. This decreases by one stitch.

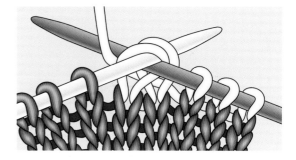

P2TOG (PURL TWO STITCHES TOGETHER)

Purl along the row until you reach the area you want to decrease. Purl through the next two stitches as though they were one stitch. This decreases by one stitch.

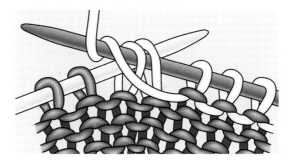

MULTIPLE DECREASES

You can also decrease by more than one stitch at a time. For example, some of the pattern instructions ask you to k3tog or p3tog. Work these decreases as explained above; you will just need to insert your working needle through three stitches and knit or purl them together as though they were one stitch. K3tog and p3tog decrease by two stitches.

Increasing stitches

Increasing stitches is where you make a stitch.

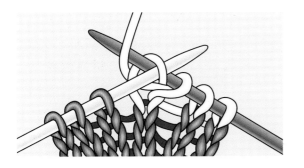

KFB (KNIT INTO THE FRONT AND BACK OF THE STITCH)

Knit along the row until you reach the stitch where you want to increase. Knit into the front of the next stitch on the left-hand needle. Instead of removing it from the needle, knit into it again through the back loop. Then slip the original stitch off the left-hand needle.

PFKB (PURL INTO THE FRONT, KNIT INTO THE BACK OF THE STITCH)

Purl until you reach the stitch where you want to increase. Purl into the front of the next stitch on the left-hand needle. Instead of slipping it off the needle, take the working yarn to the back and knit into the stitch through the back loop. Slip the original stitch off the left-hand needle.

YO (YARN OVER)

Wrapping the yarn over the needle makes an additional stitch and a hole in knitted lace and textured patterns. Knit along the row until you reach the stitch where you want to increase and make the hole. Bring the yarn over between the two needles. Knit the next stitch, taking the yarn over the right-hand needle. To make a hole without increasing the number of stitches, work k2tog instead of just knitting the next stitch.

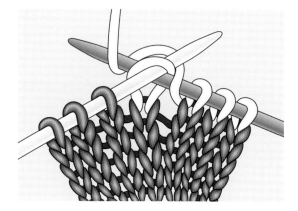

M1 – (MAKE ONE STITCH)

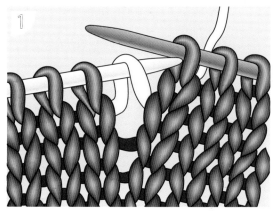

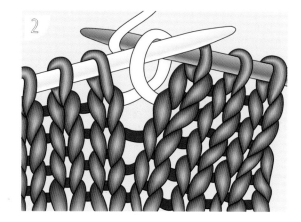

1 Knit along the row until you reach the stitch where you want to increase. From front to back, slip the left-hand needle under the horizontal strand of yarn that lies before the next stitch.

2 With the right-hand needle, knit into the back of the picked-up strand to make the new stitch.

KNITTING IN THE ROUND

Some projects in this book are knitted in the round on double-pointed needles. Some use the i-cord technique, which produces tubular pieces. Often you will want to place a marker to show the beginning of the round.

Knitting on double-pointed needles

Double-pointed needles are shorter than standard needles.

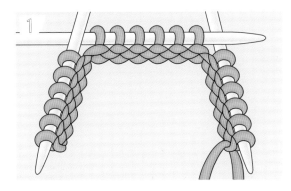

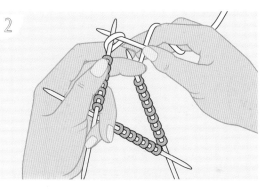

1 Cast on as normal and distribute the stitches equally over three double-pointed needles. Often the pattern will tell you how many stitches to put on each needle.

2 Using the fourth needle, knit the stitches off the first needle. This needle is now free to knit the stitches off the second needle. Continue using the free needle to knit stitches off the next and so work round and round.

Knitting i-cord

Using two double-pointed needles, cast on the number of stitches needed and knit them. Instead of turning the work, slide the stitches to the other end of the needle. With the knit side facing you, take the working yarn across the back, pull it tight and knit the stitches. Repeat this, drawing the knitting into a tube.

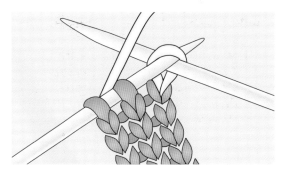

PICK UP AND KNIT

This is how you pick up stitches from a completed piece of knitting in order to work a new piece that is joined to the completed piece.

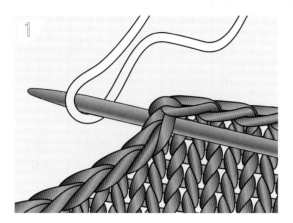

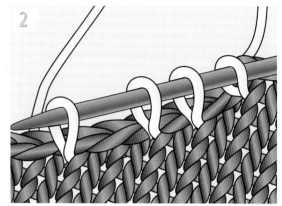

1 With the right side of the work facing you and one knitting needle in your right hand, **insert the needle tip through the knitted fabric to the back, at least one stitch in from the edge. Wrap the working yarn clockwise around the needle, as if to knit.

2 Draw this loop through the fabric to the right side of the work and leave it on the needle. ** One stitch has been picked up. Repeat from ** to **, working along the finished edge picking up more stitches. The pattern will tell you how many stitches are to be picked up.

MAKING UP

There are various ways of sewing up knitting, so use whichever you like or suits the occasion best. Always use the same yarn you knitted with so the stitches are less visible. Often you will be able to use the long end you left when you cast on. It's best to use a knitter's sewing needle with a large eye and blunt end so that you don't split the yarn.

Weaving in ends

You will have some loose yarn ends from casting on and binding (casting) off, so weave these in first. The best way to weave in the loose ends so they will be invisible is to thread the yarn end through a knitter's sewing needle and sew it into the edge of the knitting by passing the needle through the 'bumps' of the stitches on the wrong side of the work. Sew the end in for about 1–2in (2.5–5cm) and then snip off any excess yarn.

Backstitch (reverse sides out)

Put both knit sides (right sides) together so the wrong sides are facing you. Carefully make small stitches along the edge, taking the needle down for each stitch behind the end of the previous stitch. Make sure you are sewing in a straight line as close to the edge as possible. It might sound obvious, but it is very easy to pick up stitches that are further away from the edge than you think. You want the sewing to be as invisible as possible.

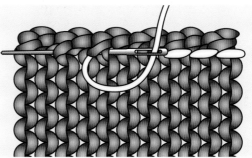

Mattress stitch (knit sides out)

Put the two pieces of knitting next to each other, knit sides up and edges aligned. Secure the stitching yarn on the back of one piece of knitting and **bring the needle up through the middle of the first stitch on the piece nearest you. Take the needle under both 'legs' of the first stitch on the other piece of knitting. Bring the needle back to the first piece, down through the centre of the stitch it came up from and up through the centre of the next stitch.** Repeat from ** to ** along the row, pulling up the stitches fairly tightly to close the seam.

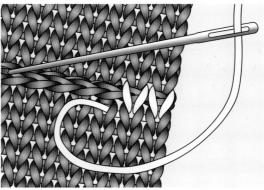

FINISHING TOUCHES

Some simple embroidery and appliqué is needed to complete some projects.

Fly stitch

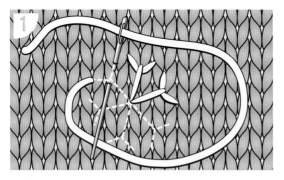 

1 Thread a darning needle with the yarn needed and insert it from the back of the work to the front at the top left of where you want the stitch to be. Insert needle at the top right of the stitch and bring it out at the top of the long central part of the stitch. Make sure that the point of the needle goes over the loop of yarn.

2 Pull the yarn through. Insert the needle at the bottom of the long stitch and pull the yarn through.

Appliqué

Use tiny straight stitches to sew the edges of fabric to the knitting. Make your stitching as neat as possible and be creative with the colour of thread. The most important thing to ensure is that the fabric is sewn securely to the knitting. Use sewing thread rather than yarn.

SUPPLIERS

Loop Knitting supplied all the yarn for this book.

LOOP KNITTING
15 Camden Passage
Islington
London, N1 8EA
Tel: +44 (0)20 7288 1160
www.loopknitting.com
ships yarns worldwide

I also used yarns from the companies listed here. Visit their websites for more information and stockists:

BERROCO
www.berroco.com

BC GARN APS
www.bcgarn.dk

CASCADE YARNS
www.cascadeyarns.com

COLINETTE YARNS
www.colinette.com

DEBBIE BLISS
www.debbieblissonline.com
(US) www.knittingfever.com
(UK) www. designeryarns.uk.com
(AUS) www. prestigeyarns.com

JAMIESONS OF SHETLAND
(US/CAN) www.simplyshetland.net
(UK) jamiesonsofshetland.co.uk

JUNO FIBRE ARTS
www.etsy.com/shop/JunoFibreArts
lilupix.typepad.com

KING COLE
www.kingcole.co.uk

PATONS
(US/CAN) www.patonsyarns.com
(UK) www.coatscrafts.co.uk
(AUS) www.patons.biz

ROWAN
www.knitrowan.com
(US) www.westminsterfibers.com
(UK) www.knitrowan.com
(AUS) www. auspinners.com.au

SIRDAR, INCLUDING SUBLIME
www.sirdar.co.uk
(US) www.knittingfever.com
(UK) www.sirdar.co.uk

TWILLEYS OF STAMFORD
www.tbramsden.co.uk

MALABRIGIO YARN
www.malabrigoyarn.com

ABOUT THE AUTHOR

Claire Garland happily lives and knits down by the coast at the far west tip of the UK in Cornwall. She lives in a little white stone cottage with her husband and three children. She is the founder of Dot Pebbles, a collection of knitted doll patterns that she sells from her website and blog – www.dotpebbles.com and www.dotpebbles.blogsite.com – and from Etsy. Claire is also a regular contributor to the knitting community site and yarn and pattern database, Ravelry.

ACKNOWLEDGEMENTS

Firstly, a huge, massive thanks to Susan Cropper at Loop (www.loopknitting.com) for supplying all the wonderful yarn for the projects in this book – her website and shop are a knitter's Utopia, a woollen wonderland!

Secondly, I could not have wished to work with a better bunch of dedicated and talented friends. The result of this book is a testament to you all. Thanks for making it work so seamlessly. I'm happy, very happy!

And finally, to dear Kate and Marilyn. Thanks for your very patient checking, proofing and amending – I know I'm in safe hands when I work with you both!

YARN INFORMATION

Each of the project instructions gives a generic description of the yarn that was used. The specific yarns I used are listed below if you want to recreate the project exactly.

Yarn companies frequently update their lines and may discontinue certain yarns or colours. If the yarns below are not available, or if you want to use a substitute yarn, you will need to work out the yardage (meterage) needed, as yarns vary. Details will be on the ball band or on good yarn suppliers' websites so that you can make comparisons.

PAGE 14: COSY COVERINGS
COSY QUILT
Rowan Big Wool: 1 ball in shade 25 Wild Berry
SNUGGLE PILLOW
Sublime Organic Merino Wool DK: 1 ball in shade 188 Tulle

PAGE 24: LOVELY LIGHTS
TASSEL LANTERN
BC Garn Allino: 1 ball in shade 23 Yellow
BUTTON LANTERNS
BC Garn Allino: 1 ball in shade 25 Light Olive
BC Garn Allino: 1 ball in shade 13 Blush Pink

PAGE 32: FUN FRUIT
PEAR DOORSTOP
Cascade 220 (Solids): 1 ball in shade 8910 Citron
PEAR PAPERWEIGHT
Sublime Extra Fine Merino Wool DK: 1 ball in shade 0106 Colonel Mustard

PEAR PINCUSHION
Twilley's Freedom Spirit: 1 ball in shade 505 Earth

PAGE 44: COOL HEAD HAT
POM-POM HAT
BC Garn Semilla Grossa Organic Wool: 2 balls in shade 112 Granny Smith
KNOT HAT
BC Garn Semilla Grossa Organic Wool: 2 balls in shade 111 Gorgeous Turquoise
BOBBLE HAT
Patons Pompero: 2 balls in shade 051 Delphinium

PAGE 52: GIVE A WAVE MITTS
WRIST-LENGTH MITTS
Jamieson's Shetland Spindrift: 1 ball in shade 525 Crimson
THREE-QUARTER-LENGTH MITTS
Jamieson's Shetland Spindrift: 1 ball in shade 470 Pumpkin
ELBOW-LENGTH MITTS
Jamieson's Shetland Spindrift: 2 balls in shade 188 Sherbet

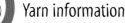

PAGE 60: TOASTY TOES SOCKS
SLIPPER SOCKS
Sirdar Big Softie Super Chunky:
2 balls in shade 330 Meringue
ANKLE SOCKS
Debbie Bliss Como: 2 balls in shade
19 Forest
LONG SOCKS
Debbie Bliss Como: 4 balls in shade
12 Red

PAGE 70: TWINKLE NECKLACE
BEADED BEADS
Juno Alice Lace: 1 ball in shade 4885
Heather Shadow
BUTTON NECKLACE
Colinette JitterBug: 1 ball in shade
167 Lavender Lil
POM-POM SCARF
Malabrigo Worsted (Aran): 1 ball in
shade Fuscia (93)

PAGE 78: FENG SHUI PURSE
COIN PURSE
Rowan Belle Organic DK by Amy
Butler: 1 ball in shade 016 Cilantro
Floral cotton fabric is Darla by
Tanya Whelen
BIG PURSE
Rowan Colourscape Chunky by Kaffe
Fassett: 1 ball in shade 434 Candy Pink
Knitted heart: Cascade 220 Solids:
small amount in shade 8910 Citron

PAGE 86: HUG A MUG COSY
TAKE-AWAY CUP COSIES
Berroco Peruvia Quick: 1 ball in shade
9119 Mostaza (coffee cosy)
Rowan Big Wool: 1 ball in shade 050
Madras (tea cosy)
Berroco Peruvia Quick: 1 ball in shade
9114 Chipotle (chocolate cosy)
MUG COSY
Debbie Bliss Glen: 1 ball in shade 02
Light Grey Melange

PAGE 94: MONSTER HAPPY
MINI MONSTER
King Cole Merino Blend 4-ply: 1 ball in
shade 5 Sky
MEDIUM MONSTER
Cascade 220 (Solids) : 1 ball in shade
2439 Gelato Yellow
MONSTER MONSTER
Malabrigo Worsted (Aran) : 1 ball in
shade 148 Hollyhock

INDEX